Her Majesty's Texans

NUMBER SEVENTY-EIGHT

The Centennial Series of the Association of Former Students

TEXAS A&M UNIVERSITY

ROBERT J. ROBERTSON

HER MAJESTY'S TEXANS

Two English Immigrants in Reconstruction Texas

TEXAS A&M UNIVERSITY PRESS
COLLEGE STATION

The paper used in this book meets the minimum requirements
of the American National Standard for Permanence of Paper
for Printed Library Materials, Z39.48–1984.
Binding materials have been chosen for durability.

LIBRARY OF CONGRESS
CATALOGING-IN-PUBLICATION DATA

Robertson, Robert J.
  Her Majesty's Texans : two English immigrants in Reconstruction
Texas / Robert J. Robertson. — 1st ed.
      p.   cm. — (The centennial series of the Association of Former
Students, Texas A&M University : no. 78)
  Includes bibliographical references and index.
  ISBN 0-89096-841-1
  1. British Americans—Texas—Beaumont—Biography. 2. Leonard,
John W. 3. Johnson, J. W. L. 4. Beaumont (Tex.)—Biography.
5. Reconstruction—Texas. 6. Immigrants—Texas—Beaumont—
Biography.   I. Title. II. Series.
F394.B3R63   1998
976.4'06'0922—dc21
  [B]   98-19819
                                                                        CIP

FOR

———————

June

Christine

Adin

Alyssa

Colin

Christian

Charlotte

Colleen

Louis

Christopher

AND

Nicholas

CONTENTS

ILLUSTRATIONS

PREFACE

Historian Charlotte Erickson has written extensively about British immigration to America, a massive movement that peaked during the nineteenth century. In her book, *Invisible Immigrants* (1972), she analyzes the experiences of British immigrants and demonstrates that many achieved quick assimilation in the United States, thus becoming "invisible immigrants." This history follows along the path of Erickson's work and, I hope, qualifies as a case study of themes suggested by her. This history also owes much to the work of Thomas Cutrer, whose *English Texans* (1985) surveys British natives who settled in Texas and outlines their contributions to the Lone Star State.

This narrative covers the experiences of five English Texans: Robert H. Leonard, Will Johnson, John W. Leonard, Hannah Leonard Lamb and her husband, Tom Lamb. But it is focused closely on Will Johnson and John Leonard, the two young cousins who came to Texas in 1869. Their letters and newspaper writings form the principal primary sources for this history. While living in Beaumont, both worked as journalists and wrote columns for the local paper. Years later John Leonard, after settling in New York City, penned some forty newspaper articles describing his adventures in Texas. Written more than four decades after the actual events, Leonard's articles must be handled with great care from a historical viewpoint. They are valuable, however, in terms of verifiable facts and with respect to attitudes, especially racial and political.

The thirty-five personal letters of Will Johnson and John Leonard have a substantial historical value. Linking together members of the English family and connecting Beaumont and London, they reveal much about these young Englishmen and their experiences in Texas. I am a great grandson of Will Johnson and inherited sixteen of these letters from my mother in 1986. The other nineteen came to hand under remarkable circumstances in 1990. That year I received a letter from Leonard D. Druce of Beaumaris, Australia, a man entirely unknown to me at the time. He explained that he was a grandson of Will Johnson's sister, Sarah Ann, and that he possessed sixteen home letters written by Johnson. I was stunned to learn of the letters and later delighted to receive copies from Mr. Druce. Reading these letters provided the initial inspiration for writing this history.

In gathering primary source materials, I have also been greatly assisted by Howard E. Tompkins of Needham, Massachusetts. The grandson of John W. Leonard, Mr. Tompkins had collected photographs, letters, and other information in preparation for writing a full scale biography of his grandfather. He freely shared these materials, and for his generosity I am very grateful.

Focused on the adventures of Will Johnson and John Leonard, this study concentrates on their activities as teachers, lawyers, politicians, churchmen, and journalists. Generally I follow Johnson's and Leonard's adventures chronologically, but in some cases I develop their stories by topic. For example, I cover all their schoolteaching activities in one chapter, even though they carried out these activities at somewhat different times. Thus, I beg the reader's indulgence when the narrative jumps ahead or backwards in time, in order to complete the discussion of a particular subject.

ACKNOWLEDGMENTS

While researching and writing this history, I have been assisted by friends and acquaintances, listed here in no particular order: Judith Walker Linsley and Ellen Walker Rienstra, who tightened up my prose and endured without complaint my sophomoric enthusiasm; Dr. Barry Crouch of Gallaudet University, an ardent disciple of Clio, who urged me to "buy a computer and write more history"; Dr. Paul Richards of Norfolk College of Arts and Technology and Pat Midgley of True's Yard Museum, King's Lynn, Norfolk, England; Dr. Randolph B. Campbell of North Texas University, who reviewed my primary materials and judged them worthy; Dr. Denis Paz of North Texas University; Dr. Ralph A. Wooster of Lamar University, my thesis professor in 1964–65, who provided encouragement and professional guidance; Dr. John W. Storey of Lamar University; David Montgomery, Joyce Rivette, and Jonathan Gerland, all of Tyrrell Historical Library, Beaumont; Kun-Woo Choi of Beaumont Public Library; Della Balsano of Brock Enterprises, Beaumont, who answered all my word processing questions; Patsy Clapper of Texas State Representative Mark Stile's office; Diane Faucher of Austin State Hospital; Thomas K. Lamb, Jr., and Jeannie Mouton Coffin of Beaumont; Bernice Giddings of Houston; Doris Cowart of Oakhurst; Kate Adams, Stephanie Wittenbach, and Steve Stappenbeck, all of the Center for American History, Austin; Charles Johnson of the Ventura County Museum of History and Art, Ventura, California; John Walden of the Beal Memorial Library, Bakersfield, California; Michael Redmon of the Santa Barbara Historical Society, Santa Barbara, California; Carol Johnson of the Texas Room, Houston Public Library; Donald Firsching of the Archives of the Episcopal Church, Austin; Robert Schaadt, Penny Clark, and Darlene Mott, all of Sam Houston Regional Library, Liberty; John Anderson and Donaly Brice of the Texas State Archives, Austin; and W. T. Block of Nederland.

HER MAJESTY'S
TEXANS

A DEATH IN CALIFORNIA

March 4, 1904, the *Free Press* of Ventura, California, published a mysterious story. The man known as James W. Leonard, the once-popular California newspaperman who had just died in the county hospital, had been identified as J. W. L. "Will" Johnson. The paper revealed the shocking news that Johnson had masqueraded for more than a decade under a false name and that earlier he had lived almost fifteen years in Beaumont, Texas. There, he had been a teacher, journalist, and lawyer, and, there, he had abandoned a wife and three children. For reasons not entirely known, Will Johnson had disappeared from Texas and surfaced later in California, where he assumed the shortened name of James W. Leonard, took a second wife, and put together another career as a writer, reporter, and publisher.

According to the Ventura paper, the mystery of Johnson's life was heightened by the pathos of his last years. Less than ten years earlier, Johnson, as Leonard, had been one of "the brightest newspaper writers . . . in the state, and at one time a high salaried foreign correspondent . . . being employed by *Scribner's* and *Harper's Weekly*." In 1893 he had married Bernice Pelham, a young schoolteacher, but within two years, she died tragically of an illness. Devastated by losing her, he had suffered a total collapse, and, the article continued, "a few months after her death, the once brilliant writer was found lying across . . . her last resting place, paralyzed in mind and body." Since that time, and for eight long years thereafter, Johnson had been confined in the county hospital, his "mentality . . . shattered, and his life, past and present, . . . almost an absolute blank."[1]

Other California newspapermen, reflecting on Johnson's lonely death, offered additional testimony about the man's talents and character. One remembered him as "an exceptionally bright newspaperman" possessed of "one of the brightest intellects." Another referred to his "wonderfully winning personality," recalling that he was "convivial, generous, clever." Alluding vaguely to "weaknesses" and "recklessness," the journalist asserted that Johnson "possessed many of those rare and dangerous qualities with which Dickens had invested the character of Steerforth in *David*

Copperfield." Few who knew him did not like him, the writer explained. "His appeal to the heart was direct and irresistible."[2]

The full story of Will Johnson's curious life, including his adventures after leaving Texas, has not yet been discovered; but much is known about his years in Beaumont. He was one of five members of an English family that came "out to Texas" during the Civil War and Reconstruction. In addition to Will Johnson, members included his uncle Robert H. Leonard, cousin John W. Leonard, cousin Hannah Leonard Lamb and her husband Thomas A. Lamb.

In Beaumont Will Johnson and the others started new lives. Capitalizing on their Victorian education and their command of the English language, they first found work as teachers and later carved out other white collar careers as journalists, attorneys, and publishers. They assimilated quickly among the Texans. The three men who immigrated as bachelors soon married American-born women; two fathered children, one siring three, the other nine. Ambitious and energetic, members of the Leonard-Johnson-Lamb clan made substantial contributions to Beaumont. Among other things, they imported various elements of their British culture, such as their English methods of education, their Victorian love of books and newspapers, and their Anglican style of religious worship.

The cousins Will Johnson and John Leonard lived in the Beaumont area from 1869 until about 1883, though John traveled in the West during 1873–77; and Will actually resided in nearby Orange, Texas, during 1879–83. During their Beaumont years, Will and John taught school, practiced law, and worked as newspaper reporters. In 1880 John began his own paper, the *Beaumont Enterprise,* which still serves the city. The same year he helped organize the town's first Episcopal congregation, founded then as the Mission of the Good Shepherd and thriving today as Saint Mark's Church. Will and John also involved themselves in Reconstruction politics. Adopting the racial and political attitudes of conservative white Texans, they helped rebuild the Democratic Party, defeat the Republicans, and thereby "redeem" the state.

While Will Johnson and John Leonard eventually moved away from Beaumont, Robert Leonard, Hannah Lamb, and Tom Lamb spent the rest of their lives there. They all found a measure of stability and prosperity in the Texas town, even though their lives were often complicated by missteps and mishaps, by illness, divorce, and money problems. But only Will Johnson committed a deed so unforgivable that he had to give up his family, change his name, and disappear from Texas; only he suffered the tragedy of death in poverty, loneliness, and disgrace.

CHAPTER 1

INVISIBLE
IMMIGRANTS

Queen Victoria's subjects were an adventuresome people; millions traveled and settled throughout the world, doing the work of their queen or just seeking their fortunes. Many traveled "out to India" and "out to Australia," and some came "out to Texas." Among those who came to the Lone Star State were five members of the Leonard-Johnson-Lamb clan. Robert Leonard migrated first, arriving in 1855 and serving as a beacon and sponsor for the others. His nephews, Will Johnson and John Leonard, followed in 1869, while his niece, Hannah Leonard Lamb, and her husband, Tom Lamb, made the trip in 1875.

In coming to Texas, Robert Leonard and his relatives were part of a massive nineteenth-century British immigration movement, in which more than ten million English made their way to the United States. Pulled to America by economic opportunities, they traveled as individuals or families, often moving along "chains of migration," within networks of friends or relatives. Arising almost entirely from the working and lower middle classes, the English immigrants found work in American agriculture, industry, and various white collar occupations, such as teaching, bookkeeping, law, and journalism. With their Anglo ethnicity, their fluency with the American language, and their familiarity with the English-based customs, they assimilated rapidly, more so than other foreigners, such as the Germans and Irish. Because of this speedy adaptation to America, the English have been called "invisible immigrants." But invisibility did not guarantee an easy transition. Unprotected by close-knit ethnic ties that characterized German and other European immigrants, English newcomers often suffered homesickness, depression, alcoholism, and sometimes severe mental illness.[1]

Most of the English immigrants settled in the East and Midwest, with only about six percent taking up residence in Texas and other Southern states. During 1860–80, when Texas enjoyed an infusion of twenty-eight thousand new families of all origins, only one half of one percent were English. The English who did come to Texas tended to gravitate to the larger towns, such as San Antonio, Galveston, and Houston, but they amounted to less than two percent of the population in each of those cities. In Beaumont and Jefferson County the picture was the same; in 1870 English Texans accounted for only about twenty out of nineteen hundred.[2]

Will Johnson and John Leonard migrated to Texas in the same year but at separate times and with different life experiences. Will was reared in King's Lynn, a provincial town of sixteen thousand, while John grew up in London, a city of three million. London was the largest and wealthiest city in the Western world—the home of the queen, capital of the British Empire, and center stage for the latest in business, industry, science, and literature. Often called "Great Babylon," the vast metropolis presented startling contrasts of poverty and luxury and, as historian L. C. B. Seaman has observed, "overcrowding and squalor co-existing with wealth, fashion, and opulence."[3]

John was born June 6, 1849. He and his older sister Hannah were among the seven children of Howard and Mary Leonard, a working class couple who lived on Seafront Street in London. Howard Leonard, a brick mason by trade, qualified as a "respectable workingman," a figure in Victorian history credited with being industrious, thrifty, reliable, and dedicated to his family. Howard earned enough money to provide a comfortable home for his family and a basic education for his children; he also imbued them with ambitions for social and economic advancement. In one generation, Howard's children would climb to the middle class; John would become a teacher, lawyer, and newspaperman, while Hannah would marry a colonial plantation manager and later work as a teacher and schoolmistress.[4]

Before coming to America, John already had seen something of the world. He quit school at age sixteen and spent several years working as a sailor and traveling to distant parts, including Australia and India. Later he returned to England where he associated briefly with a traveling theatrical group and also worked for a London paper that sent him to France to cover the 1867 Paris Exposition.[5]

John crossed the Atlantic in 1868, disembarking in New York when he was nineteen years old. He sojourned a few months on the East coast, working a short stint for a New York paper and visiting in Rhode Island. In a private home in Providence he experienced his first American Christmas, enjoying "Yankee hospitality at its best—turkey and 'fixings,' pumpkin pie and cider, good people, good fare, country dances, pretty girls."[6]

Casting about for something to do, John corresponded with his uncle, Robert Leonard, who urged him to come to Beaumont, Texas, and become a lawyer. John liked the suggestion and soon took passage on a steamship of the Mallory Line, a company that provided weekly service for passengers and freight between New York and Galveston.[7]

John landed in Galveston and promptly found transportation to Beaumont on board the sloop *Emma*. The boat was captained by James Dalton and carried two other passengers, Lem and Ed Ogden. The Ogden brothers and Captain Dalton were the first Beaumonters John met. He later recalled, "they were fine companionable men with whom I established a sincere and lasting friendship."[8]

The *Emma's* voyage to Beaumont involved an offshore leg to Sabine Pass plus a navigation up the Neches River. As they sailed through the Gulf of Mexico, "the Ogden boys exercised their privilege of pioneers to 'josh' the 'tenderfoot.'" They regaled John with tales of "man-eating alligators . . . blood-thirsty black bears, scalping Indians," but he had been initiated in Australia and did not take the bait. Instead John returned fire, telling the Ogdens "stories of Australian kangaroos and ornithorhynchuses [duckbills], Indian tigers and other fauna . . . with a slight dash of Munchausen [extravagant fictions of travel] to season." Thus the tedium of travel was lightened and "a pleasant time was had by all."[9]

When their boat neared Sabine Pass, they spotted a sudden squall moving their way, roughing the waters of the Gulf. They made it across the Sabine bar with relative ease but watched other boats that were not so fortunate. About two dozen sloops and schooners were caught in the open ocean and threatened by the mounting seas. As a group, the boats veered toward the Louisiana coast, making for a point about a mile from the pass. At that moment, he later reported, John overheard his companions talking. "That mosquito fleet is making tracks for the oil pond, eh, Jimmie?" asked Ed, as he watched the concentrated efforts of those vessels. "Yes," Dalton answered, "and they're lucky to be near it, for the squall will be heavy while it lasts." Lem asked, "What do you think causes that oil pond?" Dalton replied, "Coal oil, I reckon." John's curiosity was aroused but he said nothing, believing that the men were trying again to string him along. Later he learned the "oil pond" was a genuine phenomenon of nature, a patch of ocean so thick and sluggish with oil that boats took refuge there during storms.[10]

The storm soon passed and they continued their journey. At the village of Sabine Pass, they stopped briefly to deliver goods to a merchant, then proceeded in a northerly direction across Sabine Lake and up the Neches River. The river's course is winding and secluded, its upper reaches lined with thick timber. John was impressed, commenting that he "had sailed . . .

into many ports and various harbors, but for native beauty . . . none excelled
the unfolding panorama . . . of the tree-lined Neches." He noted the "low-
lying right bank . . . crowned by stately cypress trees, festooned with Spanish moss, and the left bank, somewhat higher and occasionally rising into
bluffs . . . covered with sweet-gum and other trees, similarly draped."[11]

As they made their way slowly up the river toward Beaumont, John must
have wondered about Uncle Bob. He had never seen the man, but knew the
broad outline of his life, from stories told by his own parents. Robert
Leonard was born in 1834, the youngest of eight children of Mary and James
Leonard, a tenant farmer at Grimston, Norfolk. His brothers included
Howard, nineteen years older, who had married and moved to London.
When Robert was only a young boy, his mother died and he was taken to
London and reared by Howard. While living with his brother, Robert re-
ceived a basic education, mastering the skills of reading and writing. But he
went to sea at an early age, probably fourteen or fifteen, thus leaving
Howard's home before John Leonard was born.[12]

In the merchant marine Robert Leonard had matured and prospered,
working his way up to become deck officer on the American ship *Wiscasset*
and later acquiring his own schooner, *Stormy Petrel.* In 1855 he sailed his
boat to Southeast Texas, settling in Beaumont where he married and
started a family. At first he supported himself by teaching school and haul-
ing freight on the *Stormy Petrel,* but later took up the practice of law, a profession in which he thrived. By the time John and Will came to Texas,
Uncle Bob was living in a comfortable house on the banks of the Neches.[13]

John arrived at Beaumont on Thursday, January 7, 1869, a mild winter
day with bright sunlight and blue skies. As Captain Dalton maneuvered the
Emma up to the Main Street dock, John saw several men, including Robert
Leonard, who watched from the shore. When the boat came to rest, John
leaped to the dock and received a warm welcome from Uncle Bob, a hearty
handshake that symbolized the older man's influence in bringing other family members to Texas. Soon, John's cousin Will Johnson would be leaving
England and heading for Beaumont.[14]

Will was born in King's Lynn, Norfolk, on September 3, 1852. He was
the youngest of three children of Thomas and Sarah Johnson; Sarah was a
Leonard from Grimston, a sister to Howard and Robert. Will was the baby
in his family by a wide margin, nine years younger than his sister, Sarah
Ann, and eleven years junior to his brother, Samuel. Given the uncom-
monly long name of James William Leonard Johnson, he was known affectionately as "Will" or "Willie" and more formally as "J. W. L. Johnson."[15]

King's Lynn, also known as Lynn Regis or simply Lynn, was a thriving market town with ancient churches, Saint Margaret's and Saint Nicholas's. Situated on the banks of the Ouse River, Lynn was a bustling port, home to numerous ships and seafaring folk. Among them was Will's father, who made a decent living as a merchant seaman. He shipped out periodically and perhaps owned fractional interests in some of the vessels. In 1861, when Will was nine, Mr. Johnson moved his family into a new brick house on Marshall Street. The dwelling was modest in proportions, only two small rooms upstairs and two down, but for a Victorian working class family was probably considered comfortable and desirable.[16]

The Marshall Street house was conveniently situated for the Johnson family, especially young Will. From there he easily roamed the town center with friends such as George Kemp, Arthur Hilling, and Martha Agger. Martha was Will's special sweetheart, a pretty girl for whom he carried a crush all the way to Texas. Will and brother Samuel attended the British School on Blackfriars Street, only three blocks from his house. Operated by headmaster Charles William Croad, the British School provided the latest in Victorian education.[17]

During the early 1860s, when Will was growing up, the people of Lynn enjoyed solid prosperity and many advantages of the modern Victorian era. Notable amenities included the Athenaeum library and arts center, the West Norfolk Hospital, and the Public Baths that offered complete bathing and showering facilities. The town enjoyed regular railroad service to Cambridge and London, plus the benefits of several newspapers. Among them was the *Lynn Advertiser,* a handsome weekly that prided itself for receiving "hot news" from London via the telegraph. Later Will would receive the *Advertiser* in Beaumont and enjoy its news of England and his hometown.[18]

Disaster struck the Johnson family in August 1866, when Thomas Johnson died of consumption. Will, then only fourteen, Sarah Ann and their mother became entirely dependent on Samuel, who had married and established himself as a teacher at the British School on Blackfriars Street. Soon, within less than three years, the Johnsons suffered dislocation again, this time when Samuel accepted a British School position in London and moved the entire family there. It was this relocation that eventually triggered Will's immigration to Beaumont. Exactly how and when Will made his decision to emigrate from England is not known, but it is clear that he went to Texas because of Uncle Bob.[19]

Will traveled to Texas in the spring of 1869, when he was only sixteen years old. He emigrated directly from the bosom of his family and unlike

WILL JOHNSON IN ENGLAND.
Author's Collection.

John had no previous experience with being away from home or supporting himself. On June 11, 1869, Sarah Ann wrote to Uncle Bob, asking him on behalf of the family to look after their youngest. "Dear Uncle," she explained, "My dear brother has come over to you" and "Mother hopes she shall not be asking too much off [*sic*] you to have an eye to him." Thus, with the simplest words, "uncle," "brother," and "mother," Sarah Ann expressed the essence of the emigrant family network.[20]

In Beaumont, Will received warm hospitality from Uncle Bob and friendly greetings from Cousin John, with whom he soon bonded. They were bright young Victorians—ambitious, energetic, and emboldened by their British education and culture. They were eager to make their way and be accepted by the local people, especially the young women. Both were small in stature, less than six feet tall, but there the similarity ended. John was spare but Will boasted a sturdy and muscular physique. John's face was long and narrow, with prominent eyes, while Will's visage was graced with more rounded and ample proportions. By John's own estimation, Will was more handsome and had greater appeal to the girls. And by general agreement, Will bore a striking resemblance to Uncle Bob.[21]

From the time of his arrival in Beaumont and for several succeeding years, Will carried on an episodic correspondence with Sarah Ann in London. He wrote to her about Uncle Bob's family and his own adventures in Texas, while she sent letters to him, and sometimes to Cousin John, informing them about family affairs in England and occasionally sending news about important events there. They traded photographic portraits, popular mementos for family members so widely separated; and also exchanged newspapers, Will sending Beaumont papers to Sarah Ann and she mailing him those from London and King's Lynn.

Will loved his family and longed to stay connected to them; he wanted the affection of his sister and mother, and the respect of his brother, Samuel. Also, he yearned for reports about King's Lynn, enjoying any news or papers from his hometown. Sometimes homesick, he pleaded in his letters for the latest about family and friends. "Tell me all the news about Lynn . . . [and] about my old classmates, where they are and what they are doing."[22]

Sarah Ann tried to keep Will posted about Lynn, in September 1869 reporting almost breathlessly about her recent trip to their hometown, where she had seen the Prince and Princess of Wales. It was "a grand day at Lynn," she wrote, for the royal couple had visited the town to dedicate the new Alexandra Dock. Named for Princess Alexandra, the dock was an ambitious project intended to make Lynn one of the largest ports in England.

The genial prince, later Edward VII, and the glamorous princess "went in state," Sarah Ann explained. The streets were all "hung with flags and the bell of Saint Margaret rang all day and the new bell at Saint Nicholas rang for the first time."[23]

At first Will addressed his home letters to "Dear Sister, Mother, and Brother," but later he restricted his greeting to Sarah Ann, a change that reflected a troubled relationship with brother Samuel. For more than two years Will hoped for a letter from Samuel; on several occasions he wrote directly to his brother, pleading for such communication, and frequently he lobbied Sarah Ann, asking her to persuade Samuel to write to him. For some reason Samuel did not write to his younger brother; perhaps he was literally too busy or maybe Will had somehow offended him before leaving England.[24]

Simultaneous to Will's correspondence with Sarah Ann, John carried on a similar exchange of letters and newspapers with his sister, Hannah, who lived in India with her husband and their children. Hannah sent letters frequently to John and sometimes to Cousin Will. She also wrote regularly to her parents in England. By these exchanges of correspondence, the Leonards, Johnsons, and Lambs carried on a triangle of communication among Texas, India, and England. Letters and newspapers went in all directions, thereby keeping intact the family network and ultimately facilitating the immigration of Hannah and her family to Southeast Texas.[25]

In Beaumont, Uncle Bob took good care of both young men, providing them food and lodging, introductions to local people, and tours around the town, such as it was. If Will and John, who emigrated from London, expected much of Beaumont, they must have been sorely disappointed. With barely a thousand inhabitants, the little town huddled on high, wooded banks overlooking the wide, slow-moving river. Frame buildings, mostly unpainted, were scattered along dirt streets. There were no schools or churches, only the two-story Jefferson County Courthouse that marked the center of town.[26]

As John recalled, it had been "three years and eight months after the close of the War Between the States," and the town was suffering "the paralysis of the so-called reconstruction era." Beaumont, like the rest of Texas and the South, was in a depressed condition; most of its white citizens were disheartened by defeat in the war and resentful of Reconstruction programs imposed by the Republican Congress. The town was occupied by Union troops, and the state was governed by Republicans—the soldiers and politicians representing for most white Beaumonters the unwelcome authority of the victors over the vanquished.[27]

Before the war Beaumont had thrived, its population growing and business expanding. With a basic economy of cattle ranching and sawmilling, the town boasted a real potential of becoming an important transportation center. Served frequently by steam boats, the town was at the junction of two ongoing railroad projects, the Eastern Texas Railroad and the Texas & New Orleans Railroad. Already Beaumont had enjoyed a working rail connection with Houston, a service that promised a rich future for the local sawmill industry.[28]

But after the war, when John and Will arrived, the town was moribund. The population had dwindled, money was scarce, and commerce was feeble. Industry was at a standstill, the sawmills idle from lack of demand and shortage of transportation. The railroad projects had been abandoned and the antebellum roadbeds allowed to wash away. The railroad bridges across the Neches and the Trinity Rivers were broken down, and there was no rail service at all, except for a handcar that carried the mail between Beaumont and Liberty.[29]

John remembered Beaumont of those days as a "muddy, isolated, somewhat somnolent hamlet," with no municipal activities or improvements, no "construction or upkeep of streets, highways, park spaces, or other public works." The streets were unpaved, though some storekeepers and householders had constructed wooden sidewalks. The people gathered water in cypress cisterns with rain guttered from roof tops. There were no drainage or sewage systems, and outhouses were seen throughout the town.[30]

The town was justifiably infamous for rain, mud, and insects. Frederick Law Olmsted, who had passed through the area before the war, told of his horse almost drowning just east of Beaumont, after a local had warned him that the road was "pretty wet." A Galveston newspaperman, Henry R. Green, poked fun at the town, calculating that the Beaumont atmosphere was composed entirely of insects, about two-thirds mosquitoes and one-third fleas. Later John Leonard himself would refer affectionately to Beaumont as "a little old mudhole" and a "lumber camp stuck in a mudhole."[31]

Uncle Bob often took his young nephews to his law office at the courthouse. The 1854 building was a simple wooden structure, recognizable by its bell tower and well known as the center of all governmental, religious, and social activities. The first floor was divided into offices, some rented to lawyers, and the second level was taken up entirely by a commodious chamber that served variously as courtroom, church sanctuary, and dance hall. The roof of the lofty chamber was supported by a massive cypress column, famous because it had withstood a direct strike of lightning.[32]

He introduced them to county officials, such as district clerk John Pipkin, deputy clerk Wilbur Gilbert, and sheriff George W. Payne. They saw John K. Robertson, the old secessionist lawyer whose "picturesque vocabulary . . . became sulphurous when anything was said about the Republican Party and its Freedmen's bureau." They met other Beaumont lawyers: James Armstrong, who was Uncle Bob's office mate, and George W. O'Brien, both of whom would become close and helpful friends. No doubt John and Will paid particular attention to the courthouse personalities, because they wanted to begin the study of law as soon as possible.[33]

In Uncle Bob's company, Will and John became acquainted with most of Beaumont's leading citizens. Among them were ranchers Moise Broussard and William McFaddin and merchants C. C. "Lum" Caswell, Samuel W. Mellon, and John C. Craig. Another retailer was Frank Herring, who ran a drug store that doubled as the post office. There were two physicians, a Dr. Watkins and a Dr. Simmons, and one minister, the Methodist John Fletcher Pipkin, who operated the town's only sawmill on an irregular schedule. Other manufacturing was carried on by the Ogden brothers, who produced cypress shingles, and by John C. Milliken and Henry E. Simpson, who constructed the popular cypress cisterns.[34]

Will and John settled comfortably with Uncle Bob, soon taking him as a role model. They followed closely in his footsteps, using their British education to obtain teaching jobs, later using those experiences as stepping stones to other positions. The young Englishmen mixed easily with the Beaumonters and soon enjoyed the company of local young women. As Uncle Bob had done earlier, they assimilated quickly, becoming "invisible immigrants."[35]

CHAPTER 2

"ANYBODY . . . CAN TEACH SCHOOL"

Soon after Will Johnson arrived in Beaumont, he wrote to his family in London about the strong likelihood of getting work as a teacher in Texas. "School teaching in this country is not like it is in England, for anybody with a moderate education can teach school."[1]

Will may have been a rank newcomer to Texas, but he was correct about the poor condition of education in the state and the opportunity for even partially qualified people to teach school. And it was a situation that he and his cousin John Leonard readily turned to good use. They had indeed earned "moderate educations" in England, and soon after coming to Texas, they found jobs as teachers, then later used the positions to enter other careers. The same procedure worked later for Will's cousin Hannah and her husband, Tom Lamb, who after migrating to Beaumont supported themselves by teaching school.

By taking up the teaching profession, John and Will followed an example set earlier by their uncle, Robert Leonard. Having learned to read and write as a boy in London, on two occasions during the 1850s Uncle Bob supported himself by keeping school before he could make a sufficient living as a lawyer in Beaumont. At one time he served as a tutor for the four children of Christian Hillebrandt, a Danish immigrant who owned a large ranch in the southern portion of Jefferson County. Later he kept a school in Beaumont where his young students included Gertrude Millard, daughter of Judge Henry Millard, and Rosalie Patridge, daughter of Jefferson County sheriff Worthy Patridge. By a curious turn of fate, Robert Leonard wound up marrying both these girls. He married Gertrude first and by her fathered two children. Later, after she died, he married Rosalie, with whom he had four more children.[2]

When Will and John immigrated to Beaumont in 1869, Texas had no real public education system. Before the Civil War, Texans had depended on an assortment of hybrid schools—private academies funded by both student tuition and state appropriations. With teachers certified by county school boards, the academies drew per capita funds from the state for the education of indigent children. But the private-public schools had been ruined by the war, their faculty and students dispersed, the state funds squandered on railroad loans or spent for military purposes. In the lean years just after the war, no state funds were available for education, and few schools were operated.[3]

An exception to this lack of formal education were schools set up by the Freedmen's Bureau, an agency created by Congress to assist African Americans in their transition from slavery to freedom. In Texas and other Southern states, the bureau organized numerous schools and furnished basic education to blacks who had been denied all formal instruction under the slavery system. Most white Texans were indifferent or opposed to the education of the former slaves, but the bureau persevered. During 1865–70, the bureau rented classrooms, hired teachers, and provided rudimentary education to more than twenty thousand black Texans.[4]

But overall, education in the immediate postwar years looked bleak. In 1870 the National Bureau of Education examined conditions in the state and found high rates of illiteracy and not one publicly supported school. The bureau called Texas "the darkest field educationally in the United States."[5]

Beaumont was a microcosm of education conditions statewide. Before the war the town had enjoyed the benefits of a bona fide private school, the Beaumont Male and Female Academy. Operated first by A. N. Vaughan and then Felix O. Yates, the Beaumont Academy had been closed when Yates volunteered for service in the Confederate army. Just after the war no real schools for whites were organized, though Vaughan did teach a few students until he found other work. The Freedmen's Bureau operated a school for African Americans in Beaumont during 1867–68. Taught first by William Lewis and later by George B. Barton, an African American, the school was a forerunner of local black schools.[6]

Will Johnson and John Leonard were able to take advantage of the Texas school shortage and find work as teachers because of the educations they had earned in England under the British schools system. The British schools were one of two major systems in England, the other being the National schools. The National schools were affiliated with the Established Church, while the British schools generally drew students and support from nonconformist congregations. The two systems were similar, except in their methods of teaching religion: the British schools provided nondenominational instruction, as contrasted with the National schools, which followed the Catechism and the Book of Common Prayer of the Church of England.[7]

Will and his brother Samuel attended the British school on Blackfriars Street in King's Lynn. There, they earned basic educations, following a standard curriculum of reading, writing, arithmetic, algebra, geography, scripture, history, and science. The school was directed by Charles William Croad, a man prominent in their town. Croad possessed a strong personality, and in his education of them he became a role model to the Johnson boys.[8]

Samuel, the older of the two brothers by eleven years, preceded Will at the school and excelled under Croad's tutelage. In 1864 Samuel worked at the school as a teacher and the next year succeeded Croad as master of the institution, holding that position until 1869. Will followed Samuel through the school, thus being taught by both Croad and his brother. Will remembered Professor Croad fondly, remarking that "he holds a high place in the rank of whom I honor and respect."[9]

John Leonard earned his basic education at the Borough Road School in London, the institution where the British system had been created and perfected. The British program employed a monitorial or pupil-teacher method, in which older students taught younger ones. Boys and girls, usually between the ages of fourteen and eighteen, taught half their time and were instructed the other half. At schools like Borough Road, student-teachers were apprenticed to adult masters, subjected to standard examinations, and required to teach a common schedule of courses similar to those offered at the school in King's Lynn.[10]

When John Leonard attended the Borough Road School, it was the largest in London, with nearly three thousand students. He enrolled there probably because of his cousin Samuel, then teaching in the British school system. Under Sam's influence, John progressed smoothly at Borough Road, though his marks were uneven. As John would later report, he "barely squeezed through in mathematics," but ranked "first boy in two and second in three of the other studies." He succeeded in the program, qualifying as a student-teacher when he was fourteen years old and teaching in the school for two years.[11]

John's success at Borough Road was due to his own abilities and to a home environment conducive to learning. In typical Victorian fashion, he and his sister became avid readers at early ages, reading books at home and those borrowed at libraries. John read family volumes by Dickens and Thackeray, and obtained others from the British Museum library. Hannah likewise consumed many volumes, including Dickens's *David Copperfield*. Ironically, this famous fictional tale, with its tragic story of James Steerforth, would later be compared to the real-life story of Will Johnson.[12]

Years later John recalled how he used his British school education to obtain a teaching job in Texas. In June 1869 while he was working in Uncle Bob's law office, alongside attorney James Armstrong who shared the quarters, the office was visited by Moise Broussard, a well-to-do rancher from the nearby settlement of Taylor's Bayou. After completing his legal business, Broussard mentioned to Armstrong the need for a teacher at Taylor's Bayou, preferably someone skilled in teaching and having some knowledge of French.[13] Armstrong called John into the office and introduced him to Broussard. The rancher questioned John about his experience as a pupil-teacher under the British schools program and in addition learned about a brief stint of newspaper work John had done at the 1867 Paris Exposition—common ground between the two, since Broussard also had attended the Paris event. He quickly offered John the teaching job and asked him to come to Taylor's Bayou two weeks later.[14]

The time between his acceptance of the position and his arrival at Taylor's Bayou were what John later described as "two weeks of terror," as he felt daunted by what seemed to him an impossible task. Broussard had told him that he would be teaching thirty to forty pupils, children of all ages, and five or six cowboys who could not read or write. Among the younger children, only a few knew any English. John's own French was not fluent and was Parisian in style, while the French at Taylor's Bayou would be of the Acadien or Creole variety. But far more serious than the language difficulties were the problems of discipline. What would he do with a bilingual group of thirty students, ages ranging from six to twenty-eight, who were not accustomed to any kind of restraint? Being only twenty years old himself, he thought he was finished before he started: "What the kiddies wouldn't do to me, the cowboys would."[15]

In spite of John's apprehensions, his cousin Will thought the job sounded like a fine opportunity. Right away he wrote to his family in England, reporting enthusiastically that John was going to Taylor's Bayou to establish a school and would probably get $2 for each scholar each month. Will did have one reservation about the proposition: he doubted John "will get much ready money for in this country they pay nearly all debts, even to school expenses in goods, cattle, horses, orders on stores, etc."[16]

Meanwhile John made preparations for his school, scouring Beaumont for supplies. He gathered up "various discarded and dilapidated *McGuffey's Readers,* a primary arithmetic or two, an *Ollendorf* French primer, pencils, crayons and other odds and ends." Then he rode to Taylor's Bayou, finding no obstacles along the way except for "an occasional young alligator" that caused his horse to shy. When he arrived at the settlement, he inspected the school, finding "a log house . . . , the roof made of rough clapboard." At first the floor was native dirt, but within a few weeks it was laid with split logs.[17]

His first day as a teacher was a Monday, "the doomsday" of his nightmares. As promised, his class comprised more than thirty students, including five cowboys, two being former members of the Confederate cavalry. Among the children ages five to fifteen, four or five had attended school elsewhere but not in several years. The others had not been to school at all, though most could speak some English "in the rural Texas vernacular." Some of the French children could write their letters and spell a few words of simple French. Nearly all the French youngsters had to be taught the English alphabet.[18]

As it turned out, his fears were groundless. "The cowboys were especially anxious to learn," he remembered. Broussard had organized their work schedules to allow the cowboys to attend school for part of the day. For them, John began by writing script samples, such as "pothooks and hangars," and started them to work. Then he turned to the children, evaluating and grouping them according to their educational needs. The process was tedious to the youngsters, and some became restless and noisy.[19] Their rowdiness disturbed the cowboys who were studying at a nearby table. The eldest, a six-foot cavalry veteran, advanced toward the youngsters and, John recalled, blurted out a stern warning: "Look here, you damned kids! Mr. Moise let us come here to learn to read and write and we've got to do it this term. If you cut up so we can't study, we'll come over there and wring your damned necks, and that goes. Savvy?"[20]

With his discipline problems solved, John was able to apply all his energies to teaching. He liked working with the children, educating them with the elements of English and penmanship and the rudiments of arithmetic. In the afternoons, when the cowboys had gone to work, he told the youngsters stories about Columbus, Washington, Lee, and other celebrities of American history. Sometimes he drew crude maps and regaled the children with tales and wonders of other lands. At recess, he encouraged them to be as noisy as they wanted to be.[21]

John found a friendly reception among the people at Taylor's Bayou, boarding around as was the custom, spending a week at a house, each with varied fare, from simple "hog and hominy" in a modest dwelling to a richer cuisine at the table of a more affluent rancher. Invited to participate in the local social life, he attended dances at the school house and admired the pretty girls. On one occasion, when torrential rains flooded the area, the cowboys and their dates had to wade through deep water to get to the school building. John remembered the girls who came barefoot with their skirts pulled high to keep them dry, carrying their shoes and stockings in bundles, then putting them on for the dance. He liked the parties, fondly recalling the "fun, freedom, and friendship." As much as he enjoyed his months at Taylor's Bayou, however, he did not remain there for a second term, deciding instead to return to Beaumont and the study of law with Uncle Bob.[22]

At the time John started at Taylor's Bayou, Will was searching elsewhere for a teaching position. In doing so he followed in the footsteps of other educational entrepreneurs who operated schools throughout the state. Many Texas schoolmen were highly mobile individuals who would move to a town to "get a school," recruiting students and drumming up support among local businessmen. Their operations blended public and private aspects of schooling; they both drew per capita funds from the state and collected tuition from their students. They gathered income, paid expenses, and kept what was left over for their salaries. Needless to say, these itinerant schoolmen lived precarious financial lives and relocated frequently in search of better situations.[23]

With help from Uncle Bob, Will got leads to teaching jobs, first in El Paso then at Oakville in Live Oak County. Finally, he secured a position in Dogtown, a tiny village on the Frio River south of San Antonio. As did John at Taylor's Bayou, Will used the British teaching program. In December 1869, Will wrote to his family and reported that he was "receiving $15 dollars per month and my board, . . . teaching on the same plan as the British school at Lynn." He also bragged he was "spoken of as the best teacher that ever yet reached Dogtown."[24]

Will thought Dogtown was a rough place, describing it to his family as a "wild and fire-eating country" and asking them to send their letters through Uncle Bob at Beaumont, because "no English or otherwise foreign letters will reach this outlandish place." He wrote to Uncle Bob, giving him news of Dogtown, asking his advice and, no doubt, asking for favors. Uncle Bob responded, pleading his own problems but promising to help him: "I do not know what to say to your questions, as I have so many in the family, but . . . I want to do you all the good I can, and anything I can do, I shall do with pleasure." He closed with sound familial advice: "Make good use of your time to improve yourself."[25]

Will was not happy at Dogtown. He complained about the low pay and, perhaps more importantly, that "there wasn't any young ladies there." Will shared his cousin John's eye for the girls. He lasted only one term at Dogtown, going back to Beaumont in May 1870 to live with Uncle Bob and teach school.[26]

Will's entry into the school business in Beaumont coincided with important developments in education at the state level. The Republican government, headed by Governor E. J. Davis, attempted to organize a new centralized public school system for the state. Implementing the educational provisions of the 1869 Constitution, the Republicans passed laws in 1870 and 1871 creating the state's first free public school system. Administered by a state education board, the new system featured compulsory attendance for white and black children, taxation of local property, and standards in textbooks, study courses, and teacher certification. All these features, now accepted as standard, were at the time considered revolutionary in Texas.[27]

But most white Texans resisted the new school system. Generally, they cared little about the education of African Americans; moreover, they would not even consider the possibility of whites and blacks attending the same schools. Many, who were generally hostile to any program proposed by Republicans in Austin, refused to pay new taxes, failed to file reports, and, over time, charged the education board with corruption, extravagance, and excessive bureaucracy.[28] Years later, John Leonard told stories ridiculing the new education program. In typical Democratic style, he belittled the Republican plan as a "carpetbag" boondoggle that "was top-heavy and unworkable." The plan went into unnecessarily bureaucratic detail, he recalled, even prescribing standard text books such as *Steele's 14 Weeks Course in Chemistry* and *Steele's 14 Weeks Course in Geology;* it was "*Steele,* steal, steal from beginning to end, like all the other operations of the carpet-bag government."[29]

In another story John joked about John Howard, a "carpet-bag" bureaucrat sent by the Republican government in Austin to inspect schools in Jefferson County. Howard was an Irishman—"educated, genial, and humorous, with a delicious brogue." John befriended the inspector but by implication belittled the man's serious purpose. The inspector "found nothing educational in the district to inspect except his salary as he received it from Austin." At Beaumont, John introduced Howard to a group of local citizens, using their former titles as Confederate officers: "Captain O'Brien," "Major McDonough," and others. "Hould on, hould on," protested the Irishman, "In the ould country a captain is a considerable . . .

man; and a colonel can have a band of music playing before his windy while he ates his breakfast. But in this country ye've only to get drunk on trainin' day and ye're a major for loife."[30]

The Republican education program did not last long. As soon as the Democrats regained control of the Texas legislature, they took steps to dismantle the plan. During the spring of 1873, the Beaumont newspaper reported the introduction of bills to abolish the unpopular Republican education bureaucracy and get rid of the hated "carpet-bag" textbooks that were "filled with atrocious misrepresentations and tirades against the people of the South." Later that year, the Republican program was demolished and the state reverted to "community schools," a provincial system in which citizens organized local schools and drew per capita funds from state appropriations.[31] The Republican program had had little impact in Beaumont, where the citizens continued to patronize various private academies. Mrs. Olivia Rigsby kept a school during these times, as did Mrs. A. E. Lynch; later their ranks were joined by Will Johnson.[32]

When Will returned from Dogtown, he opened a school in partnership with a Mrs. Neyland. They worked together to promote the enterprise and hosted a May Day party at the courthouse for the entertainment of patrons and friends. An open invitation in the newspaper promised "instrumental music, *tableau vivant,* charades, speeches, dialogues . . . a fine supper and nothing to pay."[33] Will was pleased with the party, calling it "grand" and bragging to his family in England about the theatrical farce titled "Wanted a Husband," which John had written for the occasion. Besides John and himself, the cast included the lawyer Napoleon Bonaparte Bendy and Miss Likens, a "lady friend of mine." John sang the English song "Goodbye John," and Will offered a rendition of "Captain Jinks," an American tune. The whole thing was brought off with "thunders of applause."[34]

The happy association between Will and John at the May Day celebration was indicative of their growing friendship. During the early years of their Texas adventure, they became like brothers, spending much time together, keeping in close touch when separated, and always boosting each other. The closeness of their relationship was reflected in their letters to home and in the flow of correspondence within the family network. Writing to family members, they often included news about each other's progress. More than that, when Will wrote to Sarah Ann in London, he sometimes enclosed a note from John; and John did the same, occasionally enclosing a letter from Will when writing to Hannah in India.

John and Will freely expressed their friendship and affection in letters between themselves and exchanged with other family members. Addressing each other as "your affectionate cousin" or as "Coz," the young men wrote warm and gossipy letters between themselves, trading news, joking about politics, and kidding each other about their romantic involvements. When John wrote to Will at Dogtown, he reported that his social life in Beaumont had been dull, having made little progress with the ladies. He added a hurried postscript, explaining that he suffered again from malarial fever and was "chock full of quinine," and signing off with a droll "Jolly!"[35] Apparently John had contracted malaria before coming to Texas and while living there suffered periodic recurrences, including one long bout in the summer of 1869 that left him, in his own words, "the weakest mortal ever."[36]

Will's admiration of John and his accomplishments—and the pride he took in their friendship—was evident in his family correspondence during those early years. In November 1870, while writing to Sarah Ann, Will bragged about John's progress in getting a law license and expressed genuine respect for his cousin, saying "I consider him a very good fellow."[37] Likewise, John was outspoken in his affection for young Will in his letters to Sarah Ann. John wrote to her, "I am very glad he is here for he makes me an excellent companion." In another letter, John reassured Sarah Ann about Will, promising to "render all assistance" to him and saying that "I love him dearly." He also declared that Will "is doing finely and bids fair to make one of the brightest men in the country."[38]

Will Johnson was an eager young man with an unflagging interest in women. Bolstered by his English education and manners, he was confident in his ways with girls. He flirted with many and sometimes with more than one at the same time. Believing that he should marry soon, Will wrote often to Sarah Ann discussing his marital prospects and, on occasion, describing his physical appearance. Not long after emigrating from England, he reminded Sarah Ann how he looked: "I stand about 5 ft. 6 inches, with light brown curly hair, a face naturally fair but now much tanned by exposure to the southern sun, eyes a kind of blue . . . [and a] countenance I flatter myself not altogether unpleasing." He enclosed a new portrait of himself, commenting regretfully that it was not good enough.[39]

Will's easy success with women was mentioned by John when he wrote Sarah Ann describing their adventures in Beaumont: "[Will] and I like the country and are happy and comfortable . . . [He] is an especial favorite with the people here, *especially the young ladies.*" Later, he gave details of Will's social prowess, citing a recent party at which his cousin "danced till two in the morning and just kept a going all the time," and added that Will's

WILL JOHNSON IN TEXAS
Courtesy Leonard D. Druce, Beaumaris, Australia.

"sweethearts are innumerable, which is quite natural, because he is very handsome."[40]

John and Will attended numerous parties, many in the chamber of the county courthouse. John remembered going to a ball traditionally held between Christmas and New Year's. It was the premiere social event of the year, attended by Beaumont's leading families, including the McFaddins, O'Briens, Blanchettes, Heberts, Gilberts, Ogdens, and Herrings. There were "pretty girls galore in their party frocks" and men in their best "Sunday suits." The admission price was steep and the tickets were sold at the door by Nicolas Blanchette, popularly known as "Cola" and described as "a vivacious young man with a decidedly French accent." John recalled when a youth sidled up to the door. "Mr. Cola," he asked, "can't boys come in at half price?" "Non, non," Cola replied, unfurling his answer all in one breath, "twodollar'n-half—beegleeteloldan'young." Reluctantly, the boy paid his entry.[41]

Also there were parties in private homes, Will and John often receiving their invitations by word of mouth. On these occasions, "fiddlers were numerous, amateur and unremunerated, but good at the dance music then in vogue." Among the dances were the cotillion, waltz, and polka, these more formal numbers being supplemented by spirited interpretations of "Cutting the Pigeon Wing" and "Old Dan Tucker."[42]

Vain about his appearance, Will sat periodically for photographs and sent pictures to family members and friends. On one occasion, after sending his family a recent photograph of himself, they commented that he looked much like Uncle Bob in his younger days. He basked in the warm compliment and thanked them for their observations, remarking that Uncle "is . . . considered the handsomest man in this town . . . and I believe your humble servant is said to be as much like him, excepting beard and mustache, as two peas in a pod." He promised to send more portraits as soon as he could get them taken, explaining that "the young ladies round here begged all the others from me and of course I could not refuse them."[43]

Will was pleased with the attentions of Texas girls, but sometimes he pined for Martha Agger, his former girl friend at King's Lynn. On several occasions he inquired of his sister about Martha, who "used to be my lady love when I was nothing but an unsophisticated youngster." He told Sarah Ann of wanting a portrait of Martha in order to "judge the beauty of English belles" and pondered the question of when he should marry. He needed to "decide whether or not to wait till . . . I have revisited England before I tie up my boat, hurl down my flag, and declare myself captured."[44]

Will taught school in Beaumont for at least three years, and probably more. His work as a teacher, however, was intermittent. He always closed his school during the summer because of "the great heat," and sometimes took off to engage in other activities, at one point clerking on the steamboat *Kate* and at another time working for George W. O'Brien as reporter and manager of the *Neches Valley News.*[45]

During the spring of 1873 he operated his school, advertising it as a "Public School . . . for the accommodation of white pupils." In this enterprise he competed directly with a larger school, the Beaumont Academy, at which George W. Stovall was principal. Stovall was popular in Beaumont and his school enjoyed broad public support, including endorsements from the local newspaper. Despite competition from the Beaumont Academy,

THOMAS A. LAMB
Courtesy Thomas K. Lamb, Jr., Beaumont, Tex.

HANNAH LEONARD LAMB
Courtesy Thomas K. Lamb, Jr., Beaumont, Tex.

Will continued to operate his school until 1875, when he turned it over to his cousin Hannah and her husband, Tom Lamb.[46]

Hannah and Tom had lived in India since 1868, but sometime during 1874 they decided to relocate to Beaumont. Probably they left India and came to Texas hoping to find better financial opportunities. Perhaps, like Will and John, they received a specific invitation from Uncle Bob. Whatever the particulars of the decision, their news seems to have reached Beaumont before it got to London. On December 1, 1874, Will wrote to Sarah Ann saying that "You will be surprised . . . to hear . . . that Cousin Hannah is coming out to Texas with her husband."[47]

Tom Lamb had received considerable formal education in England, having completed a primary school program and attended "college," meaning a secondary school. He also had been trained by the Toihott Indigo Company of London in the principles and practices of the indigo dye industry. About Hannah's formal training nothing is known, but it is clear that she had received a solid basic education and was thoroughly accomplished in reading and writing. She was a tireless letter writer, an omnivorous reader, and a faithful diarist.[48]

While living in India she kept a daily journal of which more than twenty-thousand words are extant. Detailing about twenty-five months of activity, the diary comprises brief daily notes covering a wide range of family, business, and social matters. The notations provide glimpses of Hannah's life as she reared her children, managed a large plantation household, and looked after Tom, who worked and traveled most of the time. Being members of the English colonial class, she and her husband participated in a continuing round of social activities: hunting for the gentlemen, croquet and cards for the ladies, and even a dinner at the house of the Maharanee to celebrate the Maharajah's birthday.[49]

But their lives in India were not all pleasure. Hannah had to contend with numerous problems, from scorpions and snakes in her house to frequent illnesses that she treated with mustard plasters, castor oil, and quinine. Also, she suffered fears and uncertainties, especially when Tom lost his original position, searched for another, and finally obtained a government job as a famine relief officer. Most of Hannah's entries are skeletal in nature and obvious in meaning. But on one occasion she recorded a thoroughly cryptic message. On October 26, 1871, she wrote out a single line: "we were alone in our glory all day."[50]

Hannah's diary contains frequent references to her regular exchange of letters with her mother in London and her brother John in Beaumont, sometimes noting that John's letters included notes from her cousin Will. On some occasions she demonstrated an interest in affairs in Texas, no doubt keeping a weather eye on their prospects in India and perhaps thinking that someday she and her husband might have to relocate. In one entry she recorded the receipt of a letter from John, with "full particulars about Texas" and photographs of Uncle Bob's family, including the newest baby, who had been named Hannah in her honor. In another she noted having received an issue of the *Neches Valley News,* the Beaumont paper that John sent to keep her informed about his adopted town.[51]

Hannah was a voracious reader, a trait common among Victorians who were committed to self-education and addicted to books, magazines, and newspapers.[52] Within a two year period she read more than ninety books of varied interest and genres. She owned books, traded books, and participated in a book club with English friends in India. She consumed dozens of romances, such as *Only Herself; The Old Love and the New;* and *Rachel's Secret,* in addition to many literary novels, essays, travelogues, and biographies. Among the authors she read were Jane Austen, Charles Dickens, Anthony Trollope, William Makepeace Thackeray, Benjamin Disraeli, Sir Walter Scott, Jonathan Swift, and James Fenimore Cooper.

Hannah read English periodicals to keep in touch with home. While in India, she and Tom regularly received the London *Weekly Dispatch* and occasionally perused other journals such as *Punch* and the *Illustrated London News*. Her cousin Will in Beaumont similarly kept up with English affairs by reading British publications.[53]

Hannah, Tom, and their three children traveled to Texas by way of England, arriving in Beaumont during the fall of 1875. They immediately followed in the footsteps of Uncle Bob, John, and Will by starting in the school business. They easily proved their teacher qualifications and were certified by the county judge to teach various subjects, including reading, penmanship, arithmetic, geography, and composition. Later, Will reported their progress to Sarah Ann: "[Tom and Hannah] are doing very well. They are teaching here and have a . . . good school. They took my school . . . when I gave up teaching."[54]

Later Hannah assumed full responsibility for the Lamb school. As did Will, she believed in the efficacy and popularity of a British education. During 1878, when she operated "Mrs. Lamb's Permanent School" for girls only, she ran advertisements in the local paper guaranteeing "a thorough English education," supplemented by instruction in "plain needlework, fancy work, and vocal music." The fashionableness of the British education was further evident at the Beaumont Academy, a competing institution that promised a similar program for both girls and boys. The proprietor declared that "discipline, impartiality . . . and thoroughness" would be used to administer "a thorough English education."[55]

CHAPTER 3

"COME TO TEXAS AND STUDY LAW WITH ME"

During 1868, when John Leonard first arrived in America and sojourned in Rhode Island, he considered various career opportunities, even the possibility of studying medicine. His uncle's letters, however, urged John to come to Beaumont and learn a profession under him. "You don't want to stay up there among the Yanks and roll pills," Uncle Bob advised him. "Come to Texas and study law with me."[1]

Will Johnson also was invited to study law with Uncle Bob. Not long after John began his law studies, Will wrote to Sarah Ann in London telling of plans to follow in his cousin's footsteps. "It will be my turn next . . . to study with Uncle." He explained, however, that because he was only eighteen years old and the minimum age for admission to the bar was twenty-one, "it will be three years before I can become a lawful lawyer."[2]

John and Will were anxious to become lawyers, since for them it would mean real advancement—young men from working-class families moving up to the ranks of white-collar professionals. The law profession offered opportunities to earn money, gain social standing, and participate in politics. In Texas, lawyers were prominent members of the state elite; they played dominant roles in business, politics, and civic affairs. Always needed to draw legal papers, they were involved in land and business transactions and often acquired substantial holdings of their own. Some were gifted speakers and proficient writers, rising in political affairs to become party leaders and elected officials. Beaumont's own George W. O'Brien was a good example of such a lawyer; a land agent as well, he gained wealth and renown as county clerk, city alderman, town booster, Democratic official, Confederate army officer, newspaper publisher, Masonic leader, and Methodist elder.[3]

It was natural that John and Will would want to follow in Uncle Bob's footsteps. The elder Leonard served as their sponsor and host, sometimes providing them lodging and helping them find work. A solid role model for his young nephews, he had immigrated to Southeast Texas on his own initiative, started from scratch, and built a decent life for himself. John ex-

ROBERT H. LEONARD
Courtesy Mrs. J. D. Giddings, Houston, Tex.

pressed genuine respect and admiration for Uncle Bob, even attributing his own record of civic accomplishments to his uncle, claiming that "whatever I have done . . . to help . . . Beaumont is due to the strong affection borne by Robert H. Leonard to his English family."[4]

Uncle Bob was a friendly and generous man whose home was a gathering place for family and friends. John recalled attending the New Year's celebration at the Leonards' house on January 1, 1870. That day the whole family was there—Uncle Bob and his wife, Rosalie, his children Jim, Alice, and "little Hannah," as well as "Aunt Harriet," their African American cook. Also on hand was an assortment of friends and relatives. At noon they gathered around the table for the New Year's dinner, a hearty feast that featured "a fine turkey and two ducks." Afterward, Uncle Bob entertained the group with his violin while John and others sang songs. In John's words, they all enjoyed "a pleasant afternoon."[5]

Robert Leonard was a talented lawyer and skilled orator who tried cases frequently in the local court. He was often pitted against George W. O'Brien, the town's best known attorney, contending with him in various civil and criminal cases. Uncle Bob was especially competent in criminal matters and handled many important cases on the criminal docket in Jefferson and Orange Counties. John described his uncle as "an able and adroit lawyer, and as an orator the most gifted man at the Jefferson County bar."[6]

According to John, Uncle Bob acquired much of his facility with the law under the training of E. A. M. Gray, a local lawyer who had died before John and Will arrived in Beaumont. Gray was known not only for his legal skills but also for his aversion to riding horses. He was famous for his habit of beginning a trip on horseback and ending it on foot, often claiming that he had simply forgotten his horse along the way. For this amusing trait the popular lawyer was fondly remembered by Uncle Bob and other Beaumonters as "Walking Gray."[7]

Will also admired Uncle Bob. Writing to Samuel in London, he boasted that "Uncle is reckoned one of the best and smartest lawyers in this country" and wished that "you could be here . . . while court is in session to hear him talk. It's bully, you bet." In a letter to Sarah Ann, Will described Uncle Bob as a powerful and dynamic man who stood 5 feet, 9 inches tall and weighed 186 pounds. Dropping into the Texas vernacular, Will called him "a Blusterer, you bet" and claimed that "a Thunderstorm ain't nowhere along side of Uncle Bob."[8]

John had taught school at Taylor's Bayou during the fall of 1869, but early the next year he returned to Beaumont to study law with his uncle. At that time Uncle Bob shared a law office with James Armstrong in the Jefferson County Courthouse. They were not law partners but Uncle Bob frequently served as associate counsel to Armstrong, who was often involved in land cases. Armstrong, John remembered, was "especially well grounded in Spanish and Mexican land law and in Texas constitution and statute law." He was "a sound lawyer" who had "little oratorical gift" but won his cases by persuading juries with his "close reasoning and confidential tone."[9]

According to John, when he started his law studies, Texas had no law schools, and few lawyers had any professional academic training. He was not entirely accurate because Baylor University at Waco did operate a law department from 1857 until 1872. But, overall, he was correct in his observation that the law profession in Texas was generally dependent on an apprenticeship system, a training method that had been inherited from England and adopted throughout the United States. Prospective lawyers apprenticed themselves to professional practitioners and learned the business by "reading the law" and by copying and rewriting legal documents.[10]

Being English and having a measure of British education had clear advantages to John and Will in the teaching business, and the same was probably true for the law profession. The Texas legal system—an amalgam of
Spanish, Mexican, and English law—nonetheless was based predominantly
on English common law. During the days of the Republic, the Texas
Congress had officially adopted the common law of England, including its
rules of evidence and procedure and use of juries. Blackstone's *Commentaries on the Common Law* (1776), a six-volume treatise on the doctrines of
English law, was considered a bible for British lawyers and likewise served
as a basic reference for Texas practitioners. Written by the famous British
lawyer William Blackstone, the *Commentaries* was studied by Texas law
students and also employed for the oral examination of lawyers wanting to
practice before the state supreme court.[11]

John's facility with the English language no doubt made him confident
of his ability to master a profession that required proficiency with words
and ideas. He apprenticed himself to Uncle Bob and Armstrong, "reading
the law" in their office and writing briefs for both. He enjoyed working on
land cases with Armstrong, who not only tutored him closely but also regaled him with "numerous stories of Texas pioneers and especially about
Sam Houston."[12]

Later, John would credit Uncle Bob and Armstrong as his "preceptors"
but claim Smith's Island as his "legal alma mater." He preferred to study his
law books early in the morning but found this impossible while living at his
uncle's house, where the children were early risers and made too much noise.
Sometimes he improvised to satisfy his need for solitude and concentration.

> When day broke, I took my books, jumped into a rowboat and drifted
> downstream until I reached Smith's Island. It was dense forest, except
> for the extreme northeast corner, where a clearing had been made equal
> to a modern residence lot. A big tree had been felled and taken away,
> leaving a wide-topped stump as a convenient settee and study. Here, ex-
> cept for once in a while a stray moccasin snake . . . , nothing occurred to
> disturb my studies. Blackstone, Kent, Story, Phillips on Evidence,
> Stephen on Pleading and dozens of other volumes studied here, struck
> deeper into my memory than any I read elsewhere.[13]

While John studied law, he clerked for a while in the hardware store of
Samuel W. Mellon, a native of Pennsylvania and uncle of Andrew Mellon,
the Pennsylvania financier who served as the U.S. secretary of treasury in

JOHN W. LEONARD
Courtesy Howard E. Tompkins, Needham, Mass.

the 1920s. John remembered Mrs. Mellon as "a lady of much charm and a leader in the Presbyterian church." On one occasion, when planning a church social, she persuaded John to stage a Texas version of "Mrs. Jarley's Waxworks," a London-style Victorian exhibition of "historical characters and malefactors of the chamber of horrors." John agreed to appear in the role of Mrs. Jarley but was troubled by his inability to impersonate the female figure or make one's self, in his words, "properly bosomed":

> The pillow suggested did not function well or feel comfortable. In those mid-Victorian days, the matter was one difficult to discuss *en famille,* but I had heard in England of a wire device called a 'palpitator,' and I spoke of it. Mrs. Mellon thought it was a great joke and was sure there wasn't anything like that in Beaumont. I sighed and said no more, but on the morning of the day for the show, Mrs. Mellon handed me the desired contraption. Mrs. Jarley herself was not better bebosomed, than I was, as her counterfeit presentment.[14]

While John made steady progress in his law studies, Cousin Will sent interim reports to his own family in London. During July 1870, he explained that John "is studying law now with Uncle Bob and expects to take out his license as a lawyer in the fall term of the court." In early November, Will wrote to brother Samuel updating the family on their cousin's progress. John "is doing first rate, he expects to get his license to practice law in a few days."[15]

Switching to a more personal matter, Will again chided Samuel about not having answered his letters. Here, the younger brother pleaded with the older for his attention:

> It has been some time since I addressed a letter entirely to you, but one of those strange ideas that sometimes flit through a fellow's brain . . . has inspired me to this. Though why it should be strange to write to a brother, I am entirely unable to comprehend. . . . I would very much like to get a letter from you; for as you know, it has always been my acme of happiness to receive a letter from Brother Sam. . . . I am so far from home & it has been so long since I left.

He closed with affectionate words. "Write soon," he implored, "and accept the kindest and dearest love of your Brother." But still his plea fell on deaf ears.[16]

In Texas a person could qualify for a law license if he had attained the age of twenty-one, resided in the state six months and had a good reputation for "moral character and honorable deportment." The actual licensing procedure involved appearing before a district judge and passing an oral examination conducted by a panel of three attorneys. In John's case, he was questioned in the Beaumont courtroom of William W. Chambers, recently appointed to the bench of the first judicial district by the Republican governor Edmund J. Davis. Governor Davis made the appointment under the terms of the new 1869 Republican Constitution that, among other things, changed supreme court and district judgeships from elective positions to gubernatorial appointments. Judge Chambers was generally unpopular among conservative white Beaumonters, because of his appointment by the Republican Davis and on account of his "scalawag" Republican politics. In this way, the justice system, as well as many other aspects of Texas life, was tainted by the controversies of Reconstruction politics.[17]

John's examination took place in the Jefferson County Courthouse on November 24, 1870. In what appears to be a classic case of a "good old boy" system at work, his examining panel consisted of Uncle Bob and Armstrong and their friend and political ally George W. O'Brien. John later described his entry into the law profession:

> I was having chills and fever, and I had to prime myself for the examination with doses of quinine . . . O'Brien asked a few questions and Robert a few—letting me down easy, but Mr. Armstrong plied me with hard ones about Spanish land law and other subjects—showing me off. But my head ached and I wished he'd quit.
>
> Then Judge Chambers took a hand and after a few minutes said to me: "Well, Mr. Leonard, if you will draw your own license, I will sign it." So I wrote it and he swore me to the usual professional oath.[18]

Employing his considerable penmanship skills, John set forth the license, then the oath: "I . . . do swear that I will support the Constitution of the United States and of this State; that I will honestly demean myself in the practice of the Law; and that I will discharge my duty to my client to the best of my ability."[19] Thus, at age twenty-one and having been in Texas for less than two years, John was granted a license "to practice as an attorney and counsellor at law in the District and inferior courts of Texas."[20]

Within a few days he was handed his first cases, having been appointed by the court to defend three men: Riley Willard and George McDaniel, both charged with theft, and Livingston Jordan, indicted for burglary. Probably all three were laborers and African Americans. John may have harbored a white Southerner's prejudice against blacks generally; but, when it came to representing Willard and the others, he apparently did the job to the best of his ability. He defended the men in Judge Chambers' court on December 3, 1870, and successfully argued two of the cases, Willard and McDaniel, before juries. A few days later he wrote to Sarah Ann, bragging about his trial results: "I was . . . fortunate to win every case, which was pretty good for a start, wasn't it?"[21]

In the case of Livingston Jordan, John had won victory for his client by persuading Judge Chambers to quash the burglary indictment that had been prepared by the district attorney, Micajah D. Priest. John described Priest as a young "scalawag" Republican from Rusk County.[22] "It gave me great pleasure to acquit my man, under the circumstances," John later recalled. "Both judge and district attorney belonged to the genus scalawag, less popular if such could be, than the carpetbaggers whose lead in political chicanery they followed." John gloated over his victory, remembering gleefully that "the favorite indoor sport of the First District bar during that period was quashing the indictments drawn by M. D. Priest."[23]

After John won their exoneration, Willard and the others were discharged immediately from custody. This outcome highlighted a slight measure of progress that had been achieved by former slaves during Reconstruction. Under the old slavery system, blacks charged with petty crimes were neither jailed nor tried in a court of law; they were simply whipped and then returned to their quarters. Now they were entitled, at least theoretically, to the same judicial treatment as whites.[24]

Soon after the court session was completed, John was sent by Uncle Bob to Bienville Parish, Louisiana, to investigate land holdings of J. D. Tarver, a dry goods retailer of Concord, Texas, who had just died. John traveled by horseback, his route taking him through the back country of Sabine County. Near nightfall he came upon a new frame residence on the outskirts of Pineville. He stopped and inquired of the homeowner about lodgings in town. The man had nothing to recommend in the town but offered John the use of his just-completed guest room.[25]

John accepted the man's hospitality, noting that he was a Confederate veteran and had a charming wife. After supper they all enjoyed "a delightful conversation about war events, literature and other topics." When John prepared to retire, his host surprised him with an extravagant claim. "'Now, sir, you are going to be the first occupant of our guest room, whose decorations represent millions of dollars.'"

> The room . . . had been recently papered, the material being entirely composed of currency of higher denominations . . . $20, $50, $100, $500, $1000 . . . being artistically laid out in geometric pattern. That it was Confederate money did not detract from its artistry. My host had been paymaster in Dick Taylor's army, and the end of the war left him with a considerable treasury . . . which he did not wish to burn up.[26]

John soon joined Uncle Bob in a partnership they advertised as "Leonard & Leonard." They offered to practice throughout the first judicial district and in the state Supreme Court. In those days, the first district comprised ten East Texas counties, including Jefferson, Orange, and Hardin, and was served by one district judge who rotated through the various counties on a regular schedule. In Jefferson County the judge held court in two-week sessions twice each year.[27]

John thoroughly enjoyed being a lawyer, especially the adventure of "riding circuit," traveling from one county to another and following the rotating court sessions:

> The practice of law . . . held the tang and the fellowship of the frontier
> spirit. We rode circuit. . . . We started in pairs but often picked up others along the road. We exchanged stories and wisecracks, and news of
> the courts, and assembled in the court rooms or at the stopping places
> and found friends in all of the county seats.[28]

In addition to Uncle Bob, Mr. Armstrong, and Mr. O'Brien, John remembered other members of the Southeast Texas legal fraternity: Stephen Chenault, O'Brien's law partner and brother-in-law, "a quiet, studious and estimable man"; John K. Robertson, "an old man . . . excitable and somewhat irascible"; and Napoleon Bonaparte Bendy of Jasper, "very intelligent and witty." Another was E. B. Pickett of Liberty, "a kindly and courteous gentlemen . . . with a fund of humor." Pickett was also known for his unusual practice of filing his legal papers in a neatly upholstered barrel; "never lost a paper in my life," he always claimed.[29]

Early in 1871 Uncle Bob arranged for John to move to nearby Hardin County and open an office for their partnership in the village of Hardin. The only lawyer in the county, J. A. Work, had recently moved away, leaving the field open. In February, John wrote to his cousin Sarah Ann, explaining, "I . . . have opened an office in the Courthouse . . . and am getting a pretty fair practice already and expect in the course of a few years to be a successful practitioner."[30]

Hardin County was a densely wooded, completely rural section in the Big Thicket region of East Texas. About four-fifths of the county was covered by heavy timber, mostly virgin pine. Logging work along with farming, stock raising, and hunting provided occupations for the people, most of whom lived on small, secluded farms. There were no towns, only two small villages: Hardin, the county seat, and Concord, a boat landing on Pine Island Bayou. At around the time John was establishing an office there, Hardin was credited by a guidebook with "an intelligent population of about 150." The little place was severely isolated; its only access to the outside world was over rough roads to the bayou or the Neches River and then downstream by steamboat to Beaumont and Sabine Pass. As one local observer noted in 1875, "we . . . never had a good road to Hardin."[31]

The population of Hardin County amounted to about 1450 people, almost all having been born in Texas or other southern states, especially

Alabama, Georgia, Mississippi, and Louisiana. Sixteen percent of the population were African Americans, among them a former slave woman whose remarkable age merited special notation by the 1870 census taker. He reported that "Hannah Arline's age is given . . . as 120 years but this is uncertain in as much she is a native of Africa." After observing that "she looks like a living mummy," he cited her sixty-five-year-old grandson, who claimed that ever since *he* had known her, she had been "too old to do any work."[32]

According to John, recreational opportunities in Hardin County were sorely limited and local men had one diversion—hunting, especially fire-hunting, which John later described:

> A lantern was fixed on the hunter's head. Deer and other animals seeing the light in the dark would stop to look at it. The hunter, looking from the darkness . . . saw the shining eyes attracted by the light. Skillful fire-hunters learned to read the shiny eyes and could with especial accuracy tell the eyes of a deer.

Not all the hunters were so "skillful." John tried fire-hunting several times but quit the sport after he bagged a raccoon and a possum and almost shot a polecat. John Dollard, the district clerk, fared even worse; he mistakenly shot and killed a blooded colt belonging to his father-in-law.[33]

Reflecting further on local conditions, John recalled, "there were no theaters or shows in Hardin County. The greatest attraction . . . was the district court, which met twice a year. . . . A large crowd came. When the matter on hand was dry and routine . . . they scattered around the courthouse square; but a jury trial packed the courtroom." People gathered from all around the county, "exchanging news on the public square or listening to the lawyers who came from the other counties of the district."[34]

John enjoyed being the only local lawyer, remembering happily that "I was alone in my glory as The Bar of Hardin County." He was hired to handle a number of cases, including one for John C. Craig, a Beaumont merchant, who was in a dispute over the ownership of some logs. Craig had bought the logs on Village Creek in Hardin County, but someone had changed their identification marks and claimed ownership of them. "I brought a proceeding for possession before a local justice of the peace," John remembered of the lawsuit. "All the logging fraternity, preparing for the spring drive, were at the trial which was somewhat hotly contested, but we proved our case and were given possession of the logs." After the trial, John talked to a lanky youth who "seemed deeply interested in the proceedings and asked me several questions about the study and practice of law." The young man, John Henry Kirby, would later receive his law license and build a fortune in the East Texas lumber industry.[35]

Even though John had moved to Hardin County in January 1871, he continued some involvement in Beaumont legal affairs. In November of that year he was indicted by the Jefferson County grand jury on a charge of perjury. Details of the case are missing, but the matter, which probably arose out of his law practice, was resolved without serious damage. He faced the charge in March of the next year when he was tried before "a jury of twelve good and lawful men," found "Not Guilty," and cleared without any fines or penalties.[36]

Making use of his spare time, John searched for opportunities in the oil business in Hardin County. Surface oil had always been visible at various points of the county, particularly at Sour Lake, and from time to time the local people experienced episodes of oil fever. According to John, during 1860–61 many oil options had been granted by land owners to developers and prospective drillers. Under these agreements, the developers were given the right to drill for oil and an option to buy or lease the land within a certain limited time, from three to five years. John believed that the life of these agreements had been extended automatically by a suspension of the statute of limitations during the Civil War. Hoping to take advantage of the suspension and make money for his clients and himself, he worked extensively with the land records and oil agreements, but produced no meaningful results.[37]

Before coming to Hardin, John's romantic attempts with women apparently were marked by a lack of self-confidence, at least he pretended so in his correspondence. He had at one time reported to Cousin Will about girl friends "Miss L" and "Ella" but expressed no optimism about his chances with either woman. "I don't think you have much to congratulate me upon in that quarter. It seems to me that I am the most unsuccessful cuss that ever was." But he had not given up, claiming that "while there's life there's hope and care killed the cat."[38]

In an earlier letter to Sarah Ann, John had praised Will as "handsome" but made fun of his own appearance. "As for me, I am getting old and ugly," he had lamented—and doubted whether he would ever find a girl. "I expect Will will be married before I am—if I ever get anyone to have me, which isn't very likely." But after moving to Hardin and playing the game of romance there, John became more confident. Writing to Sarah Ann in February 1871, he warned her not to believe what Will said about "the

Beaumont ladies being the prettiest in the world," because "the Hardin ladies beat all creation, especially one of them." The special one was Annie Livingston, and he was much smitten with her.[39]

Just a few days later, John wrote to Will in Beaumont, gossiping like a teenager about Annie and filling the letter with romantic nonsense. "Can't you just tell whoppers!" he scolded, stringing and scrawling his words as if heavily intoxicated. He claimed he had asked Annie "whether she ever did tell you any such thing as you said . . . & she said you say what aren't so and that she never did she never. I ain't going to waste any superfluous gas on you this week because you deserve to be punished for telling that all whaling fib."[40]

Annie Livingston was young, no more than sixteen, when she met John, who was already twenty-one. Born in Texas, she was the stepdaughter of Abner Brown, a Hardin County physician, who was married to Annie's natural mother, Elizabeth. Both Abner and Elizabeth were Alabama natives, though Annie's natural father had been born in Pennsylvania.[41]

Probably Annie and John were ill suited for each other. She was an inexperienced Texas country girl, while he was an educated Englishman who had traveled around the world and even lived in Paris. Nevertheless they proceeded rapidly, maybe recklessly, with their romance. On March 2, 1871, less than sixty days after he had moved to Hardin, they were married by a local justice of the peace.[42]

Soon after the wedding, John recruited Annie's stepfather, Dr. Brown, to serve as administrator in the Jacob Luder probate case, a complex matter that had far-reaching effects for all parties. Uncle Bob, as John's law partner, had just obtained a new client, James A. Stuart, a sailor based in Galveston. Stuart claimed to be the heir of Jacob Luder, also a Galveston sailor, who had died of yellow fever in 1867. Stuart had possession of Luder's bank book evidencing a $1,000 account with the Bowery Savings Bank in New York. According to Stuart, he and Luder had been shipmates, and the stricken Luder had given him the bank book and its proceeds in appreciation for caring for him in his final days.[43]

In April 1871, a curiously long four years after Luder's death, Uncle Bob and John filed the Jacob Luder estate for probate in Hardin County, allegedly because Luder had owned land in that county. John persuaded Dr. Brown to serve as administrator, a role in which he would receive and distribute the money according to the probate papers the Leonards filed at the courthouse. John would get $50, and probably Dr. Brown would receive something for his services; the rest would be divided, one third to Uncle

Bob and two thirds to James Stuart. Initially, the Luder estate looked like a profitable proposition for the Leonards; as young John naively confided to a Hardin County friend, Uncle Bob "had made a good thing out of it."[44]

At first things went smoothly; Uncle Bob ordered and received the money from New York, though it had been reduced to $850 by fees of New York lawyers. But then he refused to turn the money over to Dr. Brown, claiming the doctor had begun drinking and was not behaving in a responsible manner. Brown was mightily insulted by Uncle Bob's actions and complained to local officials, Judge William Chambers and District Attorney M. D. Priest. Brown's report to the judge touched off a storm of legal wrangling, probably intensified by political animosities between the Republican judge and the Democrat lawyers. Judge Chambers publicly reprimanded Uncle Bob and John, charging them with conflict of interest, while the district attorney indicted the Leonards for swindling and filing false papers.[45]

Upon hearing news of the charges, Uncle Bob rushed to the courthouse, surrendering the money directly to Judge Chambers, protesting his innocence, and demanding an immediate trial on the swindling charges. Uncle Bob was very upset, calling Chambers' actions "a scandal on my character." During succeeding months, he returned several times to the courthouse, pleading for a speedy trial to clear his name. On one occasion he came drunk to the judge's courtroom. Tempers flared and threats were made, but Judge Chambers maintained order, fining Uncle Bob $100 and ordering the sheriff to remove him from the courtroom.[46]

During March 1873, the case of *Texas v. John W. Leonard and Robert H. Leonard* was tried in Judge Chambers' court in Hardin County. The Leonards were defended by Captain O'Brien, the Beaumont lawyer well known for his courtroom skill and Democratic politics. In an emotional trial O'Brien dueled verbally with Judge Chambers, on one occasion causing the magistrate to become, as they said in the piney woods, "angry like a mad coon." The judge threatened O'Brien with fines and imprisonment, but cooler heads prevailed and the trial proceeded with surprising revelations.[47]

Upon giving sworn testimony, James Stuart admitted that his real name was Jaquino Adolpho Stuardo; further, much to the surprise of almost everyone in the court, Stuart explained that Jacob Luder had died and was buried under the name "Harry King." In what was a common sailor's practice, Luder had taken "French leave" from one ship and signed with another under an assumed name. Obviously Stuart's claim of the Luder money was ludicrous, if not completely bogus. Perhaps he and maybe the

Leonards were trying to obtain money that rightfully belonged to the state under escheatment laws. Whatever the truth of the matter, Captain O'Brien and the Leonards were victorious, winning a not-guilty verdict from the Hardin County jury.[48]

The Leonards escaped the criminal charges, but for John the case was a near disaster. Soon, both his marriage to Annie and his partnership with Uncle Bob were broken. Court records show that John and Annie sued each other for divorce, but indicate nothing more, not even a date. Likewise, Annie's subsequent life remains almost a complete mystery. In 1880 she was residing with her parents in Tyler County and was listed as "Divorced." Years later, when John wrote so glibly and effusively about his adventures in Texas, he never mentioned Annie, Dr. Brown, or the Luder case.[49]

While no documentary evidence has been found, timing indicates that the Luder case ruptured the Leonard & Leonard partnership. John ended his business relationship with Uncle Bob, closed the Hardin office, and returned alone to Beaumont. He roomed at the residence of James D. Bullock, a farmer and politician who would appear later in John's life. Opening his own office, he advertised himself as "John W. Leonard, Lawyer and Land Agent." Cousin Will sent a letter to Sarah Ann advising her of developments, telling her that John and Uncle Bob had dissolved their partnership. Will tried to help his cousin get started again in Beaumont. Employed then as a reporter for the *Neches Valley News,* Will touted John and his law practice to local readers, describing him as "a young man well known to our citizens for his integrity and business qualifications."[50]

John practiced law in Beaumont for a few months but then left town, as he told the story later, for reasons of health. He wrote that he reluctantly moved away from Beaumont because of a recurrence of malarial fever and upon the "insistent advice of Dr. Simmons," his local physician.[51] No doubt John suffered from periodic bouts of the fever, as did many people, but perhaps embarrassments related to Annie and Uncle Bob spurred his departure from Southeast Texas.

During 1873–77, John rambled about the West, living and working in Arkansas, New Mexico, and Arizona, even making a brief excursion to California. Becoming a kind of white-collar vagabond, he practiced law first in Little Rock, then in Santa Fe, and later moved on to Arizona where he lived for several years. There he continued in the law profession but also engaged in the newspaper business, an experience that would prove valuable when he returned to Beaumont.[52]

CHAPTER 4

HARD TIMES
IN TEXAS

On November 3, 1870, Will wrote to Samuel in London describing economic and political conditions in the Lone Star State:

> Times are awful hard now in Texas. Money is scarce, land is worth almost nothing, all private and public enterprise has been stopped and things generally are in a state of stagnation. And all this apparently retrograde movement is the result of the late war and more immediately the works of the unprincipled men, if men they are, who now hold the power in their hands.
>
> Talk of Republican freedom; it is all humbug. The Radicals or Republicans that, though in a minority, have got the power all in their hands, rule the people of the South with a despotism to which in any empire in the Eastern Continent is but child's play. They make a law to suit their party. . . . Then they carry out those laws at the point of a bayonet, for which purpose they keep large squads of Yankee Soldiers all over the country.
>
> But still I think "there is a good time coming" if we will "only wait a little longer." God will uphold the right and the next Presidential and General elections will tell the tale.[1]

Will may have exaggerated the harshness of Republican policies, but his remarks probably represented the true feelings of his uncle, Robert Leonard, and most other white Beaumonters. Like the majority of white Texans, they opposed the Republican Reconstruction programs imposed by Congress on the Confederate states, and they resented the Republican government in Austin. In addition, they looked forward to coming elections when they hoped to rebuild the Democratic Party, oust the Republicans, and regain control of their state. In the same letter, while praising a Beaumont newspaperman, Will also expressed his personal feelings about the racial question. "The Editor, Mr. W. L. Smylie, is a great friend of mine. He is a very good fellow and a true Southern white man. We term all men 'white' who uphold the supremacy of the Anglo Saxon race."[2]

Will's comments focused attention on one of the central questions of the Reconstruction period: the status of the former slaves. In the aftermath of the Civil War, Texas whites and blacks eyed each other warily; the African Americans were free from slavery, but how would they fit into the new order of things? Would the freedmen enjoy full civic and political equality in Texas? Or would white Texans impose a system of white supremacy, confining blacks to a secondary and inferior position?[3] No doubt Will considered himself "white" and longed to be "a true Southern white man." By espousing Anglo-Saxon supremacy, he aligned himself with the majority of white Texans and cast his lot politically with conservative Democrats during the Reconstruction era.

Reconstruction can be divided into four historical periods: Presidential Reconstruction, Congressional Reconstruction, Republican Rule, and Democratic "Redemption." The entire era, lasting from 1865 until 1874, witnessed a seesaw contest for political control of Texas. In simplest terms, conservative white Democrats battled against Republicans, both white and black. The Republicans captured power briefly, winning state elections in 1869, controlling the legislature for two years, and holding the governorship until 1874.[4]

Will and John arrived in Texas in 1869, at the height of Congressional Reconstruction, a period that John also explained in terms unfavorable toward the Northern radicals in Congress and their racial policies: "After the war Texas tried to function and adjust its government to the changed conditions, but the Republican extremists, under the leadership of Thaddeus Stephens [sic] of Pennsylvania and Charles Sumner of Massachusetts, were determined to force not only negro suffrage, but negro supremacy, upon the South."[5]

Stevens, Sumner, and other congressional Republicans had become dissatisfied with earlier Reconstruction programs conducted by Presidents Lincoln and Johnson. They believed the presidential programs were too lenient on the former Rebels and not vigorous enough in promoting the interests of the African Americans. They were upset by the unrepentant actions of Texas and other Southern states, which had elected ex-Confederates to high government positions, refused to ratify the Thirteenth and Fourteenth Amendments to the U.S. Constitution, and adopted "black codes"—laws that relegated the freedmen to a perpetual second-class citizenship. During 1867 the congressional Republicans undertook programs of their own to "reconstruct" the Rebel states, passing a series of Reconstruction acts to curb the power of former Confederates, advance the interests of the freedmen, and otherwise remake the political fabric of the South.[6]

To carry out these programs, Congress assumed administrative control of Texas and other Southern states, setting up military governments and granting broad powers to army commanders to carry out federal policies. General Philip H. Sheridan was given charge of the Fifth Military District, which included Texas. There, he purged the state's political system of many former Confederates, unseating all public officials who could not swear the "iron clad" oath and installing handpicked substitutes. Congressional Republicans also devised programs to change the basis of political power in the South, requiring new voter registrations that disfranchised some Confederate leaders and enfranchised all African American men. Finally, Congress required that the former Rebel states adopt revised constitutions and conduct new statewide elections.[7]

Thus, when Will and John landed in Beaumont, the Lone Star State was supervised by the army and administered by its appointees. The governor's chair was occupied by Elisha M. Pease, a Texas unionist who had been appointed by General Sheridan to replace the elected governor, James W. Throckmorton, a former Confederate military officer. Likewise, at the county level, hundreds of elected officials, mostly former Confederates who could not pass the "iron clad" oath, had been deposed from office and replaced with other civilians appointed by the military. This federal intrusion into state and county governmental affairs was resented by most white Texans and became one of their major complaints against Congress, the army, and the Republicans.[8]

During 1869 the army completely overturned the elected government in Jefferson County, unseating the sheriff, county judge, and county commissioners and replacing them with men deemed acceptable by Republican standards. Randolph W. Tevis, a member of a local unionist family, was appointed sheriff. The county judge's position was given to John H. Archer, a former Union officer and onetime agent of the Freedmen's Bureau. Born in England but having lived in the North before the war, Archer generally fit the Southern definition of a "carpetbagger"—"a northern adventurer" who came south after the war to advance himself at the expense of "gullible freedmen and oppressed white Southerners."[9]

The four county commissioners appointed by the army to serve with Archer were William Ratcliffe, born in Tennessee; George F. Block, from Prussia; W. J. Barton, from England; and S. K. Burch, from New York. All had settled in Jefferson County before 1861 and, therefore, could not be considered carpetbaggers. These men, however, along with Sheriff Tevis, did qualify for the Southern pejorative label "scalawags"—Southerners who cooperated with carpetbaggers, Republicans, and freedmen to establish a new political order weighted against ex-Confederates and in favor of Republicans and freedmen.[10]

Apparently, the "carpetbag" and "scalawag" officials of Jefferson County were reasonably efficient and gave little reason for complaint, but the mere fact of their appointment by the army was probably sufficient reason for most white Beaumonters to resent them. This resentment, along with issues pertaining to the freedmen, caused local conservatives to reorganize the Democratic Party and begin the fight to regain control of the county and state. Long time residents such as James Armstrong, W. L. Smylie, George W. O'Brien, Ed Ogden, Lem Ogden, and Robert Leonard led the way, while newcomers including Will Johnson and John Leonard played their parts. Eventually becoming known as "Redeemers," they battled against Republicans such as George W. Whitmore, Charles W. Winn, and William Chambers, men they labeled as "Radicals," contending with them for power in Jefferson County and Southeast Texas.[11]

Beaumont, the principal municipality in Southeast Texas, was a Southern town politically but unusually diverse economically and demographically. Before the Civil War the local economy had been driven not by cotton but by ranching, sawmilling, and railroad construction. With regular steamboat connections to Sabine Pass, Galveston, and New Orleans and with two ongoing railroad projects, the community had been substantially influenced by non-Southerners. In 1860, more than twenty-five percent of Beaumont's population had been born in Northern states or European countries.[12]

Despite the diversity of their business and population, however, Beaumonters had been committed to the Southern way of life, including its distinctive feature: slavery. On the eve of the war, Jefferson County citizens owned 309 slaves, employing them as sawmill and railroad workers, farm and ranch hands, and domestic servants. Beaumonters passed city laws to enforce the institution of slavery, and, when the system was threatened, they voted decisively in favor of secession. Many local men served in the Confederate army, including George W. O'Brien, William A. Fletcher, and Robert Leonard.[13]

Uncle Bob had earned solid Southern credentials. He migrated to Beaumont five years before the war, married a Texas woman, and settled comfortably among the people of Jefferson County. He did not own any slaves himself, but like most white Beaumonters supported the Southern way of life and favored the continuation of the slave system. When the war came, he enlisted in the Southern forces, serving first as a private and later as a second lieutenant in Company F of the 5th Texas Infantry of Hood's Brigade.[14]

After the war Uncle Bob became close friends with James Armstrong, who would share Bob's law office in Beaumont and serve as a mentor to Will and John. A well-known East Texas politician, Armstrong had gained political prominence in Texas during the days of the Republic and early statehood. But, as had Sam Houston, he opposed secession and during the war had joined neither side. After the war, in the early stages of Congressional Reconstruction, Armstrong had reasserted himself politically, becoming one of only twelve conservative Democrats elected to the Constitutional Convention of 1868–69. While serving in that body, he led the conservatives in their largely futile struggles against the Republicans and their policies.[15]

In December 1869, just months after Will and John settled in Beaumont, they witnessed the defeat of their friend Armstrong in his bid for a seat in the U.S. House of Representatives. They both admired Armstrong, and John described him as "an opponent of the oppressive Republican reconstruction measures and a champion of white supremacy."[16] Running as a Democrat in the East Texas First Congressional District, Armstrong had lost the race to George W. Whitmore, a Tyler County lawyer who had evolved in recent years from a staunch unionist into a Radical Republican. Armstrong carried Jefferson County by a substantial majority, but in his district-wide victory Whitmore was aided by the temporary disfranchisement of Confederates and strong support from the new African American voters.[17]

Probably voicing sour grapes, John claimed that, although Armstrong had actually won the contest, "enough votes were thrown out to give Whitmore the position." He protested further about the denial of the ballot to Rebel leaders: "Ex-Confederates were disfranchised. . . . I, having arrived in the county since the war, had a right to vote under the law, which at the same time disfranchised the best and most capable of the native element."[18]

The subject of voting must have been of great interest and satisfaction to John and Will. Had they remained in England, where suffrage was substantially restricted, they could not have voted until they qualified by means of owning or renting property of certain minimum monetary value. But in Texas, one was eligible to cast a ballot after living in the state for one year and in the county for six months and attaining the age of twenty-one. To young men having recently emigrated from England and eager to participate in politics, the advantage of Texas over England was obvious.[19]

The 1869 elections, in which Whitmore defeated Armstrong, marked high water for Republicans statewide. Aided by the restructured electorate, they garnered three out of four congressional seats, both Senate positions, and working majorities in both houses of the Texas legislature. They also won voter approval of a Republican-crafted state Constitution that centralized power in the governor's hands and confirmed enfranchisement of all African American men.[20] The governorship was captured by Texas' most prominent Republican, Edmund J. Davis, a Texan who had served in the Union army and led the Radical faction in the 1868–69 Constitutional Convention. Running against Andrew J. Hamilton, a moderate Republican, Davis won by a slim margin, 39,901 to 39,092, having benefited from a low turnout among white voters and a large vote by black Texans.[21]

But the Republican victory was not complete; moderates and conservatives won positions in various parts of the state. In Jefferson County, for example, conservatives won a majority of the important local posts. The new sheriff and Will's future brother-in-law, Edward C. Ogden, and the new presiding chief justice, Napoleon Bonaparte Bendy, were members of the Democratic Party or soon would be. And this was just the beginning; for the balance of the Reconstruction period, a coalition of Democrats and moderate unionists governed the county. The local area, including Beaumont, thus escaped most of the strident politics and civic violence that plagued other parts of the state.[22]

The election of 1869 was an extraordinary political event, the first in which black Texans voted for county and state officials. About 49,500 freedmen had been registered under army supervision during 1867–68, and approximately 37,000 had cast ballots for delegates to the 1868–69 Constitutional Convention. In the 1869 elections, African Americans voted heavily—and generally in favor of Republican candidates. While the race of voters in that election was not recorded, it is accepted widely that most blacks gave their ballots to Davis, thus assuring him of his narrow victory and making him dependent upon their support. In this way Davis became the "scalawag" governor, or so he was dubbed by Texas conservatives.[23]

The Davis victory, with its reliance upon the freedmen's vote, drew the attention of white Texans to the controversial issue of black suffrage. Only a few years before, the African Americans had been slaves, mostly illiterate, uneducated, and without civic or political experience. Now, through the intervention of Congress and the U.S. Army, they had voted in large numbers and in effect elected the governor. In addition, blacks themselves had won various county and state positions, including seats in the Texas house and senate. Among the black senators were Matthew Gaines from Washington County and George T. Ruby of Galveston, the latter a vigorous leader who wielded substantial influence within the Davis administration and the Republican Party.[24]

In the eyes of most white Texans, the rapid empowerment of the freedmen was truly revolutionary. Like the majority of white Southerners, they favored white supremacy and opposed black suffrage, believing that African Americans were unprepared for the exercise of equal political rights. Of course, black Texans considered these racial attitudes grossly unfair. Naturally, they wanted the right to vote and other privileges of citizenship, such as education, family security, land ownership, occupational independence, and justice in the courts.[25]

In Jefferson County, where since 1860 the total population had stagnated at about 2,000, the number of African Americans was growing, increasing in ten years from 309 (15 percent of the total population) to 498 (26 percent). Probably the freedmen were coming to Beaumont because of job opportunities in local sawmills. Led by men such as Woodson Pipkin, Jackson Flowers, and Bill Martin, African Americans organized their own schools and churches. They also politically asserted themselves, generally voting and cooperating with the Republicans. But they did not have enough ballots to control elections or win political offices for themselves.[26]

During these times, relations between Beaumont's whites and blacks were uneasy, but did not devolve into riots or other outbreaks of racial unrest that occurred elsewhere in Texas. The town did not completely escape racial violence, however. During 1866, three years before Will and John landed, Henry Bullock, a white saloon keeper, had murdered Jackson Northweather, a freedman. According to witnesses, Bullock attacked Northweather without provocation as the black man passed innocently through the center of town. Bullock raised his pistol and, in his own words, shot the freedman "just to see him kick."[27]

Will and John became ready converts to the Southern idea of white supremacy; they probably had been conditioned to this prejudice in England, where Victorian culture included a pronounced streak of racism. Great Britain, the world leader in the antislavery movement, had abolished its African slave trade in 1807 and had eliminated slavery from its colonies in 1833. But British opposition to slavery did not imply sympathy or respect for the black African. Most Victorians harbored strong prejudices against blacks, believing they were unprepared to participate as equals in society. On racial questions arising out of the American Civil War, Victorians generally sided with white Southerners. They conceded the need for modest changes in the South, granting basic education and limited civil rights to the freedmen, but they rejected the idea of African American suffrage.[28]

Will's and John's prompt adoption of the racial attitudes of white Texans was consistent with the practices of other English immigrants in America. Generally, those who settled in the North before the war had sympathized with the Republican antislavery cause, while most who immigrated to the South, such as Uncle Bob, had adopted Southern ways, frequently acquiring slaves and giving their support to the Confederacy. Apparently, it was often a case of "when in Rome. . . ."[29]

John recorded his initial experiences with the American freedman:

> I made my first acquaintance with the southern negro . . . when I came here. . . . Wilse Gaynor was a good fiddler and an amusing character and he and Martin Thomas, who later became a skilled sawyer at the Reliance Mill, were the two negroes I saw most of. Wilse did odd jobs around our place, and came to my uncle for advice and help on many occasions.

In typical Southern fashion, John ridiculed Wilse, in this instance making gentle fun of his ignorance and manners of speech.

> Wilse was fond of big words which he mixed up and at times invented, and he and Mart Thomas were always arguing. When they reached an argumentative impasse, they came to our office for an arbitration. I remember one occasion when they came together, and addressing my uncle, Wilse began: "Mr. Bob, me and Mart's had a sputement, an' we come to ax you to transmire de difigglety." Bob "transmired" whatever it was and sent them away satisfied.[30]

Whether expressed gently or harshly, the racial prejudice harbored by John and Will was common among white Texans and significantly influenced their political opinions. Most white Texans resented the coalition of Governor Davis and the Republicans with black voters, and it was probably this linkage more than anything else that caused white conservatives to brand their opponents as "Radicals" and to castigate them as "scalawags" and "carpetbaggers." John and other Democrats used the terms indiscriminately, often applying "carpetbaggers" to all white Republicans, even though most did not meet the definition as Northern-born newcomers.[31]

Under the leadership of Governor Davis, the Texas legislature convened on February 11, 1870, and soon passed measures required by Congress to bring the state back into the Union. It adopted the Fourteenth and Fifteenth Amendments, the former guaranteeing citizenship to the former slaves, the latter granting suffrage to all adult black males. With these and other steps, Texas completed the process of Reconstruction and was officially readmitted to the Union on March 30, 1870. The period of Congressional Reconstruction in Texas thus came to a close, and the Republican administration began.[32]

During the first two years of his administration, Governor Davis enjoyed considerable success. Teamed with Republican legislators, he obtained passage of laws designed to carry out Republican policies and to improve conditions in Texas. Texas adopted various programs aimed at economic development, such as those promoting railroads, frontier protection, immigration, and homesteading. A free public education system for white and black children was established. Under the governor's leadership, the Republican-led legislature also passed laws creating militia and state police groups for the control of violence—a complex and controversial problem arising from lawlessness, racial hostilities, and political disputes.[33]

Republicans charged Democrats with using murder, arson, and other forms of violence to intimidate their voters, especially the freedmen, and to otherwise influence the outcome of elections. Conservatives in some counties had indeed organized groups such as the Ku Klux Klan, which harassed Negro voters and, in some instances, killed black and white Republican leaders. As one modern historian noted, "hundreds died at the hands of the unreconstructed." On several occasions during 1870 and 1871, Governor Davis mobilized militia units to restore order and protect African Americans against the attacks of white rioters. Democrats likewise claimed abuse at the hands of the Republicans; they reported cases of Radicals using intimidation and violence against their party leaders and voters, including a political riot in Galveston in 1872 that Will would witness and describe.[34]

Most white Texans resented all the Davis programs, particularly the creation of the militia and the state police, both of which enrolled African Americans as members. They claimed that Republican reports of civil violence were exaggerated and that the military groups were actually created to oppress conservative whites and promote the power of the Republicans and the freedmen.[35] In typical Democratic fashion, John discounted the need for extraordinary law enforcement measures, as he described his own near participation in a unit of the Davis militia in Jefferson County:

> There was a law passed by the legislature by which each county was to organize a company of militia. More than one company was to be organized in Jefferson County, so the order came from Austin. So in compliance with the order we met and organized a white company; and a negro company was also organized. Confederate soldiers were not eligible . . . Lawson Gray was to be a lieutenant and I was selected as orderly sergeant. Governor Davis was to designate the companies to be mustered in. He ignored our white company, but recognized the negro company which, however, failed to carry on.[36]

Under the terms of the 1869 Constitution and with the blessing of the like-minded legislature, Governor Davis wielded broad new powers of appointment, handpicking various state and county officials who traditionally had been elected by the people. Included were supreme court justices, district judges, district attorneys, and election officials. The centralization of these appointive powers into the hands of the governor was resented by most white Democrats, becoming one of their major complaints against Governor Davis and the Republicans.[37]

In Jefferson County, Governor Davis appointed Charles W. Winn to the position of registrar of voters. Winn, an Arkansan who had served as an officer in the U.S. Army, had moved to Sabine Pass after the war; there he joined political forces with the freedmen and worked to promote himself and the programs of Davis and the Republicans. By these actions, Winn qualified himself as a "scalawag," even though John Leonard branded him a "carpetbagger," condemning him as "particularly obnoxious because of his endeavors to stir up race trouble in Southeast Texas." In addition to obtaining the voter registration post for himself, Winn persuaded the governor to appoint other Republicans to the election board of appeals. Among the appointees were Bosen Godfrey, a local freedman, and Edward Fink, a former New Yorker who headed the Union League at Sabine Pass. The Union League, also known as the Loyal League, was a nationwide Republican organization, the purpose of which was to enroll and motivate black voters.[38]

Winn, who published the Radical newspaper *Sabine Pass Union,* served as the chief spokesman for the Republicans in Jefferson County. He helped organize a Beaumont chapter of the Union League and through that group attempted to use the voting power of freedmen to facilitate Republican control of the area. Writing to Republican government officials in Austin, he complained bitterly about the opposition of local conservatives. He claimed that many local Democrats, including James Armstrong, were actually members of the Ku Klux Klan and were working to prevent the freedmen from full enjoyment of their rights, including a proper education.[39]

Another Davis appointee who riled John was William M. Chambers, the Chambers County lawyer selected by the governor in 1870 to be the district judge in the Beaumont area. A former slaveowner, secessionist, and Confederate soldier, Chambers abandoned the Democratic Party after the war and joined the forces of Davis and the Republicans.[40] John heartily disapproved of Chambers and his political flip-flop, ridiculing him as a classic "scalawag": "William Chambers, when the war was looming in 1861, was the wildest 'Secesh' voice in Chambers County and offered to provide enough rope to hang every Union man in the county. After the war, he took the ironclad oath and landed the judgeship of the First Judicial District."[41] Despite the fact that Judge Chambers worked regularly with Jefferson County lawyers, and even approved John's admission to the bar, he was generally unpopular among local conservatives and was subjected to repeated attempts to unseat him.[42]

Most whites in Southeast Texas believed that the administration of Davis and the Republicans represented unwarranted and unacceptable federal interference in state and local affairs. Soon after the election of 1869, the conservative whites of Southeast Texas began work to "restore home rule" and "redeem" their state, directing their principal efforts at rebuilding the Democratic Party and defeating the Republicans at the polls.[43] In Jefferson County, the journalistic spokesman for the Democrats was Will's friend W. L. Smylie, publisher and editor of the *Neches Valley News*. Carrying the banner for the party, his paper proclaimed itself to be "The White Man's Organ for the First Judicial District," with a two-fold platform: "White Supremacy" and "Subordination of the Military to Civil Authority."[44]

Smylie displayed a harsh attitude toward Republicans generally and against the Loyal League particularly. In one article, titled "Loyal League Hunter," he blasted an unnamed "carpetbagger" who was in town searching for "a position in the Bureau of Immigration, the Bureau of Education, or some other excrescence of the Radical state carcass." Allowing no possibility that the newcomer might have legitimate motives, Smylie excoriated the man as one of "the New England buzzards with which the South has been so much infested of late": "He was prepared to teach all the occult and patent sciences, many languages, the art of humbugging and cajoling the colored people. . . . He also professed to be a preacher of the Gospel . . . Get ye hence, Satan! ye owl! ye vampire! ye buzzard! to your dark lantern resorts. Beaumont is too honest for your sort."[45]

Priding himself on being the voice of the Democrats, Smylie thanked his subscribers and advertisers for their support, noting that the paper was read by more than five hundred families in eastern Texas and patronized by merchants in Sabine Pass, Galveston, and New Orleans. Lamenting the loss of official printing business to Republican papers, he rationalized the setback on the grounds of having "done right" and not aligned himself with the Republicans: "We are willing to be the White People's Journal of our district, and let the Radicals have the state patronage, and feel nothing is lost by the arrangement. We only desire that every Democrat who is able will subscribe to our paper."[46]

Rebuilding the party was the key to restoring "home rule," and Smylie covered the process closely. On May 27, 1871, he reported the recent actions of the Beaumont Democratic Club, a group of thirty-five local leaders who published and endorsed the entire platform of the state Democratic Party. In addition to Smylie himself, the club's membership included James Armstrong, George W. O'Brien, Ed Ogden, Lem Ogden, and Robert Leonard. Will and John were not listed among the Democratic leaders, but their sympathies cannot be doubted, and before long they would take their parts in revitalizing the party.[47]

The Democratic platform, a lengthy document with more than twenty declarations and resolutions, pledged loyalty to the U.S. Constitution and the national Democratic Party, then set forth the party's case against the Republicans in Austin, charging them with a long list of "high crimes and political misdemeanors." Among these were violation of the Constitution, usurpation of power, suspension of civil rights, excessive taxation, waste of public funds, corruption of the press, and subversion of elections.[48]

On the critical issues of race relations and black suffrage, the Democrats published contradictory positions in Smylie's newspaper. On one hand they acknowledged the termination of slavery: "The abolition of slavery as a result of the war is accepted as a fixed fact, and it becomes our duty . . . to provide for the security and well being of all classes of men, native or foreign born, white or black."[49] On the other hand, the Democrats claimed for Texas an exclusive right to regulate suffrage. In a classic manifesto of state rights, the white Texans implied that the state had the power to curb voting by the freedmen: "The powers of the General Government are restricted to the express grants in the Constitution, and all powers not granted are reserved to the states and the people thereof. [Therefore,] the regulation of suffrage and elections belongs to the respective states; and any interference ... by the General Government is a gross usurpation of power.[50]

The Democrats invited "all good men, whatever may have been their political preferences, to unite with the Democratic party in removing from place and power those who now control the State government." With this call, the conservatives in Jefferson County and across the state geared up for future contests against the Republicans.[51]

The Democrats had their first chance to restore "home rule" during the special elections of 1871, when four congressional seats were contested. In the second, third, and fourth districts, Democrats John C. Connor, Dewitt C. Giddings, and John Hancock ran against Republicans Anthony M. Bryant, William T. Clark, and Edward Degener. In the first district, which included Beaumont and Jefferson County, William S. Herndon, a former Confederate officer and conservative Democrat from Tyler, challenged incumbent George W. Whitmore, the Republican who earlier had defeated Beaumonter James Armstrong.[52]

Smylie roused the Democrats in Jefferson County. He attacked the Republicans and their government in Austin, declaring that "the people of Southeast Texas have done handling political issues with gloves and intend to do their share in tearing down and uprooting the government policy implemented by Eastern fanatics."[53] The Democratic cause in Southeast Texas was bolstered further by another local newspaperman, W. F. McClanahan, publisher of the *Sabine Pass Beacon*. Pulling in tandem with Smylie, McClanahan praised the Democrats and described their battle against the Republicans in grandiose terms as "justice and right arrayed against treachery and villainy. . . . loyalty and patriotism against corruption and plunder."[54]

John Leonard supported Herndon and accompanied him on a campaign swing through Southeast Texas. This was a head-to-head battle, with Herndon and Whitmore making joint appearances. After making their speeches in Hardin and Beaumont, the two candidates and their supporters boarded the steamboat *J. L. Graham* and headed downriver for a campaign rally in Sabine Pass.

Among those on board were George W. O'Brien, the Beaumont attorney; Colonel Napoleon Bonaparte Bendy, the Jasper lawyer "famed as the most accomplished raconteur in East Texas"; and Miss Amelia Gilbert, "one of the most attractive young ladies of that day." John recalled that Bendy, about seventy years old, entertained the crowd with many droll stories and then turned his attention to Miss Gilbert, whose first name he could not recall.

> "Miss Gilbert, what is your Christian name?"
> "Guess; but I let you know that it begins with A and ends with A."
> "Why, Assafoetida, of course!" said Bendy, and as the crowd roared, added, "but a rose by any other name would smell as sweet."[55]

When the boat docked at Sabine Pass, they were greeted by a large crowd of local citizens. Stepping forward, Captain O'Brien presented the Democratic candidate. "Captain William H. Herndon, Democratic candidate for Congress is here . . . to address you." The people, already friendly to the Democrats, welcomed the announcement with loud and continuous cheering. Then, the Republican Charlie Winn called out, "Honorable George W. Whitmore, our present congressman, is also here to address you." This declaration the crowd greeted with profound and awkward silence. Finally, one of the local rustics groaned: "We-ell, put him ashore, then!"[56]

The crowd reaction at Sabine Pass turned out to be a harbinger of the coming elections. In the vote of October 3–6, 1871, the Democrats swept all four congressional seats, with Herndon decisively defeating Whitmore. Whitmore polled more votes than he had in 1869, but Herndon won a clear victory, carrying Jefferson County by two to one and the district by more than five thousand.[57] John remembered the Herndon victory as a real turning point for the Democrats. "Success in the . . . congressional campaign marked the beginning of the end of the carpetbag government in Texas," he recalled. "The spirit of lethargy which had come with the loss of power to shape their own destiny was shaken off, and progress, with increasing impetus, animated the good people of Texas." Of course, in John's eyes "the good people of Texas" were the conservative whites.[58]

CHAPTER 5

"DEMOCRACY ALIVE—
RADICALISM DEAD"

Heartened by their victories in 1871, the Democrats pressed the campaign for complete "redemption" of the state during 1872–73. John and Will worked for the cause, assisting Uncle Bob and other local Democrats in their efforts to defeat the Republicans and reestablish conservative control in Southeast Texas. John served as a party official, and Will applied his hand as a partisan newspaperman. In obtaining these positions, they probably benefited from Uncle Bob's connections, in addition to their own literacy and education. As with teaching and practicing law, they gained political opportunities through their abilities with the written and spoken word; fluency with the language was a key to politics.

Direct participation in politics was a new and exciting adventure for the young Englishmen. Had they remained in Great Britain, it is unlikely they would have had such experiences, especially while still in their early twenties. For Will, the son of a merchant seaman, and John, the son of a brick mason, America was indeed a land of opportunity.

Will went to work for the Democratic *Neches Valley News* during 1872, at the very time George W. O'Brien succeeded W. L. Smylie as the paper's publisher. Will became closely associated with O'Brien, sometimes even rooming at his employer's house. Much influenced by O'Brien, Will became directly involved in Democratic politics.

Captain O'Brien, as the prominent Beaumont lawyer and politician was known popularly, had migrated from Louisiana to Texas during the 1850s. He established himself politically before the war, serving in Beaumont as both county clerk and city alderman. He opposed secession but later served willingly with the Confederate forces. After the war, he first steered a moderate, nonpartisan course but by 1872 committed himself to rebuilding the Democratic Party and ousting the Republicans. Assuming a leadership position with Democrats, O'Brien became one of the principal "Redeemers" of Southeast Texas.[1]

While working for O'Brien, Will first tasted the newspaper business and

CAPTAIN GEORGE W. O'BRIEN
Courtesy O'Brien Family Collection (MS-108),
Tyrrell Historical Library, Beaumont, Tex.

found it much to his liking. He wrote news stories and sold advertising, developing newspaper skills that later would sustain him and give him purpose. On several occasions, when business and politics took O'Brien away from Beaumont, he promoted Will to acting editor and publisher. On July 27, 1872, he printed an announcement confirming the arrangement: "During our absence, this office will be under the direction of J. W. L. Johnson, who is authorized to perform all functions and duties pertaining to the same, and to do all business connected therewith."[2]

Will responded eagerly and accepted the challenge. "We are come," he declared happily. "We were waiting for the Senior [O'Brien] to give the signal; he has given it, and we are along side, working in the same trace, pulling the same load, and let us hope, working and pulling to victory and the people's weal."[3] In the same issue Will touted the *News* as "the cheapest, best and most popular newspaper of Southeast Texas," inviting potential customers to "roll in your subscriptions."[4]

Will wrote to Sarah Ann in London, pleased about his new responsibilities with the newspaper: "I sent you a paper last week and shall do so again this week. You will perceive that I am left in entire charge of the office and you will thus see that I am getting a good reputation as a writer and editor."[5] In another letter to his sister, he reveled in his good fortune and engaged in sophomoric introspection: "Captain O'Brien is away and I have been running the paper alone for about a month. Just think of it, your young rascal of a brother, who used to be so careless, editing a paper all alone. I am proud of my abilities; I know that I have got the head and brain and also the ambition and therefore all else that is needed to make one successful is perseverance and energy."[6]

On a less happy note, Will returned to the subject of the unexplained estrangement from his brother, a condition that he now believed would become permanent. For more than two years he had waited in vain for a letter from Samuel. Now, writing to Sarah Ann, he tried to close discussion of the subject.

> I do not think of Samuel in a harsh manner, only in a sorrowful one, for he is still my brother, although he has lost the love & respect he used to get from me. I shall not mention him to you again & I do not wish to see his name in your letter until he has actually written and posted a letter to me. . . . If he does not want to write, I don't give a wit, & don't want him to write. I can paddle my own canoe, without his help or his letters. Let him go his way & I go mine. Oceans divide us and an impassable barrier lies between his heart . . . and mine. . . . I have made enough advances & now I shall await his actions. If he is content to pass on through the world as though he had no brother—so am I.[7]

During Will's several tenures as manager of the newspaper office, things sometimes went awry. On one occasion, he was surprised by an unannounced visit from J. B. Likens, a Houston lawyer who was an investor with O'Brien in the ownership of the newspaper. In a "Local" column bearing his byline, Will boyishly confessed his embarrassment: "[Likens] being one of our bosses, we felt rather bad about the scattered condition of papers and things; but his hearty laugh and pleasant talk soon made us forget that, and if he noticed the confusion, he didn't let on, and that was sufficient for us."[8] But all in all, Will was pleased with his accomplishments and charged with excitement about his future. Writing proudly to Sarah Ann, he pondered on what it might bring:

> Well . . . I am still "strutting and fuming my walk upon the stage of life," but whether I am so acting my "piece" that when "the curtain falls"

I shall slink away amid hisses—"horrible to ears refined," or walk tri-
umphantly amid the cheers and applause, to that great mysterious future,
to which we soon or later must all sojourn, is a question that I must leave
for others to say. . . .[9]

Little did he know then that later he would indeed "slink away amid
hisses—'horrible to ears refined.'"

Will did not devote all of 1872 to journalism and politics. He also spent
time romancing the local girls and reporting to Sarah Ann about his progress.
On Valentine's Day of that year, he had received twelve letters from Texas
girls and had sent out about the same number, including one with an original
sonnet to Martha Agger at King's Lynn. A few weeks later, he wrote to his sister describing his frenetic courting of not one but two young women. The
first he identified only as "a certain beautiful young lady" whom "I often go
to see" and could probably win "by playing the game of love artfully and
skillfully." The other was Viola Ogden, "a lady from Kentucky, pretty, gay,
young," who "receives my visits graciously and is my constant companion
to church and parties." Viola was the one he would later marry.[10]

Viola was well liked by Uncle Bob and his family, and she enjoyed a certain social standing in the town. The daughter of the late Dr. Frederick
Ogden, a physician and lawyer who served in the Congress of the Republic
of Texas, Viola was born in Beaumont in 1847 but was reared in Kentucky
by relatives after the deaths of her parents in the 1850s. When Will met
Viola, she had just returned to Beaumont to live with her brothers, Lem and
Ed Ogden, the same men John had met on his first trip to Beaumont.[11]

Will kept Sarah Ann posted about Viola and the other ladies, once commenting philosophically on having been rejected by one of them: "I love her
still and always shall but I am not going to run crazy over any of them. Your
brother . . . is as good as any of them, and those that affect to look down will
find that it is a case of diamond-cut-diamond."[12] In the same letter, composed
over several days, he asked again about Martha Agger and furnished news
about recent dates with Viola. He had visited her Saturday "after dark" and
the next day escorted her home after Sunday school and church. He closed
his letter Monday, remarking that Viola had joined the church on Sunday and
noting regretfully that because the church—probably Methodist—prohibited
dancing, "I shall never be able to dance with her again."[13]

That summer he became much enamored of Viola and contemplated
marriage. Realizing that he had been too cavalier about the subject in the
past, he pleaded with Sarah Ann to believe him. "I am speaking this time se-

riously and earnestly. I have put joking aside. . . . I love one girl really, truly, deeply, and fondly and she loves me too. . . . I speak of . . . Miss Viola Ogden. . . . Could I tell you the one half of my love, it would take all the words . . . of the English tongue." With tender feelings, he described his sweetheart, "her pretty figure, blue eyes, light hair, and the smallest hands and feet, a clear bright intellectual face." Noting her grace and modesty, he claimed that "her voice, sweet, clear and soft falls upon the ear like the singing of the brook."[14]

He courted Viola "artfully and skillfully," taking advantage of his British-ness and sharing with her English newspapers such as the *Illustrated London News* and the *Lynn Advertiser*, so that she could see "scenes of my youthful home." Reviewing with her his hometown newspaper, he likely re-galed her with tales of his boyhood in King's Lynn, probably boasting of his friendship with Professor William Croad and perhaps teasing her with sto-ries about Martha Agger. Showing her the London paper, lavishly illus-trated with romantic and fashionable images, he could tell about the greatness of England and hopefully gain standing in her eyes.[15]

Will busied himself working for the paper, sometimes traveling to nearby cities to collect news and sell advertising. At Galveston he capital-ized on his British background, bragging to Sarah Ann that he had come through with "flying colors" thanks to "my English education, manners . . . natural good sense, and . . . a sort of devil-may-care, easy style of talking and acting." He may have two-timed Viola with a Galveston woman, with a wink reporting to his sister that he had "very pressing and *real* invitations to visit again soon" but warned her not to mention the subject in her letters. In the same letter he enclosed the latest photograph of Viola, calling her "the best and sweetest girl in Christendom."[16]

Working as Captain O'Brien's first assistant at the *News*, Will helped campaign for the Democrats. Initially, O'Brien and Will continued Smylie's twin themes of white supremacy and subordination of military to civilian au-thority. But later, apparently believing that Texas Democrats had already proven themselves to be champions of white supremacy, they found it expe-dient to soft pedal the racial issue. They eliminated the strident racism and promised "exact justice to all and oppression to none."[17] Proudly claiming to be "A Democratic Organ," the *News* published a sixteen-point platform for the party. Among its planks were resolutions in favor of sectional recon-ciliation, a return to constitutional government, subordination of the mili-tary, just taxation, protection of the ballot box, economical education for all the people, and abrogation of the state police.[18]

In June 1872, Will took the helm of the paper and managed the operation when Captain O'Brien attended the state Democratic convention in Corsicana. O'Brien served as the delegate from Jefferson County, while Hardin County was represented by Cousin John. Having practiced law in the village of Hardin, John apparently had earned the confidence of local Democrats and been elected as their official delegate.[19]

The Corsicana convention attracted a record attendance of more than 750 delegates. With the town overflowing with visitors, John and Captain O'Brien were fortunate to find lodgings together with a Dr. Watkins, formerly of Beaumont.[20] The convention brought together virtually all the prominent Texas Democrats, including former governors Francis R. Lubbock and James W. Throckmorton, ex-Confederate leaders Ashbel Smith, Moses Austin Bryan, and John Reagan, and Congressman Bill Herndon. United in their condemnation of the Davis Republicans, the Democrats endorsed their own 1871 platform and called for an end to federal interference in the affairs of the state.[21]

Gearing up for the fall elections, the Democrats passed resolutions endorsing and nominating various candidates. For the position of state representative from Southeast Texas, they endorsed Uncle Bob's longtime friend James Armstrong. For two newly created at-large congressional seats, they selected Roger Q. Mills, a former secessionist and Confederate from Corsicana, and Asa H. Willie, a popular Galveston lawyer and businessman. John was personally acquainted with "Judge Willie" and took pleasure in seconding his nomination; when John rose to his feet, the convention chairman recognized him as "the gentleman from the free republic of Hardin."[22]

The Democrats at Corsicana spent most of their time discussing the coming presidential election and debating the wisdom of endorsing the candidacy of Horace Greeley. A prominent New York editor who favored rapid reconciliation with the South, Greeley led a Liberal Republican ticket against U. S. Grant, the Republican incumbent. For the Democrats nationally and in Texas, the Greeley-Liberal Republican ticket offered an opportunity, even if a slight one, to unseat President Grant and his Republican administration. As John recalled, "it was realized by us that a straight Democratic ticket would have . . . no more chance than a traditional snowball in Hades."[23]

Captain O'Brien favored the Greeley proposition, but John spoke and voted in opposition. Then, when the measure carried, John joined the majority in favor of Greeley to make the action unanimous. With that question decided, the Texas Democrats proceeded to select delegates for the upcoming national Democratic convention at Baltimore. O'Brien was chosen as a delegate along with more prominent party members such as Ashbel Smith and John Reagan.[24]

The Texas Democrats then traveled to the Baltimore convention and there cooperated with the national party in pledging support to Greeley's Liberal Republican ticket. While Captain O'Brien attended the national convention and lent his support to the Greeley movement, Will covered the events in the Beaumont paper.

Reporting local reactions to the Greeley proposition, Will told his readers about a recent meeting of the Sabine Pass Democratic Club. There party members had pledged their support to Greeley, believing that his election would result in "a return to Constitutional government and relieve the country from the tyranny and despotism of Radicalism, Stealicanism and Grantism." He also interviewed Maj. J. C. Blackman, a Democratic leader from Sabine Pass, who visited the newspaper office. In Blackman's opinion, the local people were much opposed to "the frauds and iniquities of the Radical ring" and unified in support of Greeley, "thinking that the action of the Baltimore Convention was the best that could be done in the present state of affairs."[25]

In Beaumont, Will found that opinions on the Greeley nomination were sharply divided. Covering the subject, he attended a Democratic meeting at the courthouse chaired by Uncle Bob and featuring a debate on the Greeley issue. Speaking in favor was Major Blackman and presenting the contrary view was J. K. Robertson, a crusty old Beaumont lawyer who opposed any compromise of Democratic principles. Robertson argued that "the Baltimore Convention had sold out, not the Democratic party, but themselves. What could be said of Grant could equally as truly be said of Greeley, and he put them . . . in the same pot, for to his mind, Greeley was no better than Grant."[26]

While covering the Greeley campaign, Will visited Galveston and recorded a very unusual story. He told of a political riot in which a mob of black Texans attacked L. D. Miller, "the colored Democratic orator from Jefferson," who was attempting to speak against the Republicans and in favor of Greeley's Liberal Republicans. In reporting this event, Will assumed a typical Democratic viewpoint, blaming white Republicans and demonizing their black associates. Miller, according to Will's story, had tried to address a campaign rally on the evening of October 21, but had been hooted down and driven from the scene by "whiskey-infuriated demonic negroes" who were "instigated and encouraged by rascally white Radicals."[27]

Three days later Miller appeared at another Galveston political rally, this time secure in the company of Democratic leaders such as Richard B. Hubbard, Democratic elector, and C. M. Winkler, chairman of the Democratic Executive Committee. Speaking to the friendly crowd of "four to five thousand," Miller urged his fellow black Texans to support Horace Greeley, "their life long friend" who "will accord them all their rights and lead them from liberty to prosperity." He also addressed himself to white Texans, reminding them of "the creditable conduct of their slaves during the war" and advising them to "shake hands with the black man and to pursue a course of reconciliation and peace."[28]

In addition to his serious reporting of the Greeley nomination, Will also printed anecdotal stories dealing with the issue. One such story that favored Greeley employed racial stereotypes, making fun of an imagined African American youth's manner of speech but crediting him with quick common sense.

> A small darkey with an armful of eight-day pups, accosted a gentleman on Pine street a few days ago with the query.
> "Want any pups dis marnin?"
> "What are they, Greeley or Grant pups?"
> At a venture the young fancier responded, "Grant."
> "Don't want'em."
> A day or two later the boy made another attempt and was asked the same question, to which he replied, "Greeley pups."
> "Why you little rascal, didn't you offer the same pups to me a few days ago as Grant pups?"
> "Das so, but dey's done got their eyes open since."[29]

When Captain O'Brien returned from Baltimore, he stopped a few days in Galveston, attending to business, speaking at a Democratic ratification meeting, and residing at "the good old Washington Hotel." From there, he transmitted to Will a lengthy report of "the great Democratic Convention of 1872." For Beaumont readers, O'Brien reviewed the pros and cons of the presidential proposition, then concluded that the endorsement of Greeley was "the only course left which will relieve us of the oppression and woes of another four years of Grant's dictatorship." He urged that all Democrats, "horse, foot and dragoons . . . shall, ignoring the past, look only to the future and give us solid, united support for Greeley."[30]

In the 1872 general election the national Democratic strategy to replace

President Grant with Greeley failed miserably. "Grant was the easy winner, . . . the plurality being 782,891," John explained, adding parenthetically that "Grant was a poor president though a distinguished soldier." He dismissed Greeley as "a doctrinaire having little acquaintance with executive matters."[31] But Texas Democrats were otherwise very pleased with the election results. Greeley did carry Texas, 66,455 to 47,426, an outcome that demonstrated the rapidly growing strength of the Democratic Party and a profound shifting of state political power. The Republican vote, believed to be mostly black, had remained stable at about 45,000, but the Democratic ranks were growing steadily, swelled by ever-increasing white emigration from other Southern states. The "redemption" of Texas by white conservatives was at hand.[32]

In fact, the Democrats enjoyed sweeping victories all across the state. Asa Willie and Roger Mills easily won the at-large congressional seats, defeating the Republican nominees, A. B. Norton and L. D. Evans, by margins of more than 5,000 votes each. James Armstrong of Jefferson County won election to the state House of Representatives, his victory being one of many that gave the party complete mastery of the house and effective control of the senate. Thus the Democrats defeated the Republicans and effectively restored their version of "home rule" in Texas. The only remaining Republican vestiges were various executive and judicial officers whose terms had not yet expired, such as Governor Davis who faced re-election in the fall 1873.[33]

Assuming control of the thirteenth legislature, the Democrats proceeded to dismantle most of the Republican programs. They repealed the state police act, restricted the governor's use of the militia, and greatly reduced the appointive powers of the governor. For example, they eliminated the appointed position of county registrar of voters, officially assigning that responsibility to district clerks and thereby canceling jobs held by Davis supporters. By this action, Charlie Winn, the Republican leader of Jefferson County, was deprived of his registrar's position and his influence greatly reduced.[34]

As discussed earlier, the Democrats passed a series of new education laws that decentralized the public school system and shifted control to an array of community schools. In addition, they called a general election for December 3, 1873, the day they planned to oust Governor Davis and finish their "redemption" work.[35]

Wanting to purge the judiciary of Republican influence, Democratic lawmakers laid plans to oust the thirty-five district judges who had been appointed to eight-year terms by Governor Davis. In reality, the Democrats proceeded selectively, taking formal action against only thirteen and unseating only four. Among those targeted for removal was William Chambers, district judge in Southeast Texas. James Armstrong, the newly elected representative from Beaumont, helped draft an impeachment resolution, charging Chambers with "embezzlement, perjury, corruption and oppression." Galveston and Beaumont newspapers applauded the initiative, the former scoring Judge Chambers for "his vindictive partisanship and intolerable tyranny upon the bench" and the latter announcing gleefully but prematurely that the "once mighty judge of the First District . . . is dead."[36]

Earlier John had denounced Judge Chambers as the worst kind of "scalawag"; now he added his voice to the cry for the judge's impeachment. He penned a long poem, "Oh, Righteous Judge!" that appeared on the front page of the Beaumont paper. In sixteen rhyming stanzas, he damned the judge while pretending to praise him, in one instance blasting him for his cowardly desertion of the Democrats and his self-serving conversion to Radicalism: "Six months a Radical, and then we see / A Judgeship given for apostasy; / And now he sits in high judicial place, / Self-chosen champion of the Afric race." Charging the judge with abuse of power, John's poem recalled the Hardin County dispute in which Chambers threatened to disbar him and Uncle Bob.

> A young attorney too, that I once knew,
> A kinsman had that was a lawyer too;
> The older one, presumptuous, did aspire
> To controvert the Judge—thus roused his ire
> Against these two uncouth, degenerate souls,
> He threatened to strike them from the rolls
> The elder one, for his presumptuous sin,
> The youth, for being, to his uncle, kin!

John wound up his roasting of Chambers, consigning him to the darker reaches. "We hope he'll have a bench when he a shade is, / He'll make a bully judge down there in Hades!"[37]

Later Judge Chambers would be brought to trial before the Texas senate on thirteen articles of impeachment, six pertaining to the notorious Jacob Luder case in Hardin County and the related dispute with Uncle Bob and John Leonard. Judge Chambers, an able courthouse lawyer, defended himself skillfully, winning acquittal on all charges, and was discharged by a unanimous vote of the senate. But the judge did not completely escape the anger of the Democrats; soon he was almost beheaded jurisdictionally, when the Texas house redrew the lines of his district, taking away all his southeast Texas counties except for Orange County. From this action Uncle Bob, John, and other local Democrats derived at least partial satisfaction.[38]

During the summer of 1873, John left Beaumont, traveling out of the state and removing himself from Texas politics. Uncle Bob, Will, and other Democrats, however, kept their eyes fixed on the coming election, when they planned to defeat Governor Davis and drive out the last of the Republicans. In Jefferson County the Democratic campaign was promoted by the *Beaumont News-Beacon,* a newspaper resulting from a merger of O'Brien's *Neches Valley News* and McClanahan's *Sabine Pass Beacon.* Edited by McClanahan and plainly labeled "Democratic," the new paper covered the party's preparations for the impending contest.[39]

On August 29, McClanahan reported a recent "Democratic Meeting of Jefferson County" that brought together all the leading local Democrats, including himself, Armstrong, O'Brien, J. K. Robertson, Napoleon Bendy, and Lem and Ed Ogden. Uncle Bob was elected chairman of the meeting and Will, receiving his first party position, served as secretary.[40] Although only a minor job, it positioned Will where he wanted to be: on the team with Uncle Bob and the other senior men, particularly the Ogden brothers, with whom he had a growing relationship because of Viola.

The Jefferson County Democrats elected delegates to the district convention at Hardin and the state convention at Austin. Robert Leonard, James Armstrong, Ed Ogden, and J. K. Robertson were among those selected for the Hardin meeting. Uncle Bob was also chosen as a delegate to the Austin convention, along with McClanahan. Emphasizing their desire for fiscal retrenchment, the local Democrats directed Uncle Bob and the other state delegates "to vote for no man for office who is in favor of granting money subsidies to railroad companies or other private corporations."[41]

The call for financial conservatism was echoed in the "Proposed Democratic Platform" that was also published in the Beaumont paper on September 29. Drafted by forty-one prominent Democratic legislators and recommended by them for adoption at the upcoming state convention in Austin, the platform favored "an immediate return to an economical administration of government." It included planks calling for promotion of immigration, fair and equal taxation, and reform of the public education system. There were no overt statements of racism, but the doctrine of state rights—particularly with regard to the sensitive issue of suffrage—was still carefully spelled out. "All powers not delegated to the federal government by the states are reserved to the states, or to the people," the Democrats declared. "The question of suffrage and the regulation thereof belongs to the states."[42]

C. M. Winkler, chairman of the Democratic Executive Committee, addressed an open letter "To the Democracy of Texas"—here, "Democracy" meaning the Democratic Party. Announcing that the state convention would be held in Austin on September 3, he urged continued vigilance, reminding party members of progress already achieved, elections won, and long-sought changes accomplished. "Civil government is fast replacing military rule . . . the half civil, half military, half savage body . . . called the state police no longer lords it over the people."[43]

In the same issue, McClanahan praised area Democrats and urged the party toward final victory over the Republicans: "We are glad to see the Democrats of this district are alive to their interests and mean business in the coming campaign. Let our organization be thorough and complete and let us pull together for a . . . decided victory over our enemy. . . . Let our delegates bring out sound and true men . . . and then let every Democrat to a man support the nominees."[44]

As the Beaumont editor had recommended, the Democrats brought forth men deemed "sound and true" by their party delegates. Meeting in Austin on September 3, 1873, the Democratic state convention drafted a slate of proven conservatives. For governor the party nominated Richard Coke, a Waco lawyer and former supreme court justice, and for lieutenant governor, Richard B. Hubbard, an antebellum Democratic leader and former Confederate army officer.[45]

During the fall of 1873, Coke and the Democrats campaigned aggressively against Governor Davis and his party, reiterating all their complaints against their opponents. They charged the Republicans with fraud, corruption, extravagance, and excessive taxation and blamed them for "the unseemly advances of the Negro." Branding Davis as "a scalawag usurper" who had been elected by "mean whites and ignorant negroes," the Democrats accused the governor of having instituted a reign of "universal terror" carried out by "paid mercenaries" and "sable supporters."[46]

As McClanahan had hoped, conservative Texas voters responded to the Democratic call. On December 3, they delivered a crushing blow to Davis and the Republicans, with Coke winning 93,682 to 45,670 votes. As with the elections of 1871 and 1872, the Republicans proved formidable, but this time the Democrats produced even larger numbers of new voters. As one writer has noted, the "massive influx of Southern white immigrants" had "rendered the outcome all but inevitable." Thus the conservative white Democrats completed their "redemption" of Texas.[47]

In Jefferson County, where Will and John had labored on behalf of the Democrats, the election results were likewise very satisfying to the conservatives. In the state races Coke and the Democrats rolled up large majorities, while at the county level conservatives and moderates again won the principal positions. With these outcomes, the local Democrats restored "home rule" in Southeast Texas and destroyed the influence of the Republicans. The Radical George Whitmore had been defeated, the "carpetbagger" Charlie Winn turned out of office, and "scalawag" Judge Chambers would be confined to Orange County until the end of his term.[48]

"Redemption" of course was a disheartening setback for black Southeast Texans such as Wilse Gaynor, Jackson Flowers, Bill Martin, and Woodson Pipkin; their hopes for political equality were dashed and their share of the American dream was denied. But local white conservatives, including Captain O'Brien, Representative Armstrong, Uncle Bob, Will, and the Ogden brothers were very pleased. On December 4, 1873, the day after Coke's election, they applauded the headline of a conservative Galveston paper: "DEMOCRACY ALIVE. RADICALISM DEAD."[49]

CHAPTER 6

"THE BEST AND SWEETEST GIRL IN CHRISTENDOM"

Will Johnson liked the idea of falling in love and getting married. This was a typical attitude for an Englishman of the Victorian age, when love was romanticized, women were idealized, and Christian marriage was considered the only legitimate venue for the enjoyment of sexual relations and the procreation of children. The family was held in high esteem, and the traditional roles of men and women were widely accepted. Husbands were cast as breadwinners and decision makers, while wives were seen as homemakers and compliant companions. This was the kind of family in which Will had been reared and the kind he observed at Uncle Bob's house. No doubt he imagined a similar life for himself.[1]

By the beginning of 1873, Will had fallen deeply in love with Viola Ogden and was determined to marry her. She was older than he by five years, but in his mind she was indeed "the best and sweetest girl in Christendom." Fair with blue eyes, she had a petite yet womanly figure. Also, she enjoyed a measure of prestige in Beaumont. Frederick Ogden, her late father, had been prominent in the town during the 1840s, and her brothers, Lemuel and Edward, were up-and-coming businessmen and political figures. Uncle Bob and Aunt Rosalie were especially fond of Viola and had recently given her name to their newborn daughter. Uncle Bob likely advised Will that Viola would make an ideal wife.[2]

Will courted Viola cleverly. Near midnight on March 19, 1873, on the eve of her twenty-sixth birthday, he composed an ardent love letter for her. "Darling," he wrote, "may this day . . . be to you one of sweet joys and pleasures. One, whose remembrances shall be full of peace and love." He wished her a long life and many years of happiness but then alluded to the melancholy fact of death, the time when she must pass the "Rubicon of life." Quoting from Ecclesiastes, he referred to the end of life when "the silver cord be loosed and the golden bowl be broken." Then he pledged his love:

> Darling . . . speaking the true wish of the innermost recess of my heart, how can I help telling, reiterating, the fond words of my love, wherein the ideal world of happiness is made strangely, dearly, truly, happily real. And that love, which overwhelms me so entirely, is poured out to you, at your mercy and controlled by you alone.

With an eerie but confused sense of prophecy, he foresaw the ultimate failure of their relationship:

> I am from the intensity of that self-same love afraid of the future. Why I know not. And from the very idea of losing you and your love I shudder. Only I pray to you, my Darling, that come what may, trample "not under your feet the heart that loves you better than anything else in the universe—better than life and its hopes of heaven."

Laying bare his soul and confessing to past indiscretions, he also spoke optimistically of the future:

> Look through the dim vistas of past years. . . . Regrets lie abundantly, lavishly scattered upon the past pathway of my life. But for one year you have made my life happier, brighter, more worth living for. Tell me how it is with you. The future is all gilded over with imagined and anticipated joy for me. It is so for you?

He returned to the birthday theme, concluding his letter with professions of love: "Again I wish you joy and many happy returns of the day of your birth. Oh! my Darling, my heart is with you, my thoughts are of you, my dreams are about you. God be with you. My heart embraces you—its idol."[3]

Signing the letter "Your own, Willie," he added two postscripts, one pleading for an answer to his letter and trying to draw her into a more intimate relationship. "I would love to receive some few words from you, but if they are to be restricted by conventionality, t'will not be what I seek. Let them—if any—be words from your heart, not the lips." In the other postscript he noted, "I send you Vashti," adding coyly, "with this recommendation—don't read it." Probably this was Augusta Jane Evans's new romantic novel, *Vashti; or Until Death Us Do Part* (1869), a flowery and heart-rending Victorian tale in which the heroine cannot return her suitor's love, due to her personal honor and Christian morality.[4]

There is no record of Viola's reaction either to *Vashti* or the love letter. She was probably flattered by allusions to a beautiful woman who demonstrated honor and integrity, and more than likely she was attracted to Will. Even though he was so young, he offered much both as a lover and prospective husband. He was handsome and confident, spoke with a charming English accent and had already demonstrated talents as a teacher and newspaper writer. Additionally, he enjoyed the status of being sponsored by Bob and Rosalie Leonard and associated with prominent men such as George W. O'Brien and James Armstrong. Every indication was that he would become a future leader.[5]

Whether Viola's brothers, Lem and Ed, approved of Will is not known. But she needed their permission to marry. She was their baby sister and probably was dependent on them for financial support. She had just turned twenty-six, while Lem was twenty-eight and Ed already thirty. They all resided in one household: Viola; Ed, a confirmed bachelor; and Lem, his wife, Cynthealia, and their two-year-old son. After the Civil War, Lem and Ed had come back to Beaumont, started in the shingle and lumber business and established themselves in local politics. In 1869, Ed had been elected sheriff of Jefferson County. By early 1873, when Will was courting their sister, the Ogden brothers had become leaders in the Jefferson County Democratic Party. In September, just a few weeks before the marriage, they all attended a Democratic meeting in Beaumont, an assembly in which Uncle Bob served as chairman and Will as secretary. Lem and Ed must have known Will and probably liked him, at least in the beginning.[6]

Will married Viola on October 28, 1873, in a ceremony conducted by Reverend John F. Pipkin, the popular Methodist minister who presided over most local weddings and funerals. Will spoke the solemn vows, taking Viola as his wife—"till death us do part."[7] Beyond these few facts, nothing else is known about the wedding affair. They likely married in a private home, either the Ogdens' or Leonards', because there was no church building in Beaumont at the time. Also, assuming the match had won general approval, it is probable that the bride was given away by one of her brothers and that the festivities were attended by Uncle Bob, Aunt Rosalie, and all their children, along with close associates such as O'Brien, Armstrong, and Napoleon Bonaparte Bendy.

For Will, getting married was a fairly simple step, but supporting a wife, and later children, proved a more difficult task. Earlier he had earned money working as a teacher and more recently as a journalist, but his newspaper job had vanished in late 1872, when O'Brien gave up control of the

VIOLA OGDEN JOHNSON
Author's Collection.

paper. During the summer of 1873, in addition to his political activities, Will had returned to school teaching, and probably continued in that profession on an intermittent basis for the next few years. He may also have "read the law" in Uncle Bob's office, since he still aimed at being a lawyer. Later, in 1877, he would go back to the newspaper business to supplement his income.[8]

Soon after getting married, Will took another legal step; he became a naturalized citizen of the United States. This was a judicial process in which foreigners were made the "same" as natural born citizens and thereby granted basic rights to vote, hold public office, and serve on juries. Available to men only and carried out in a variety of federal and state courts, the procedure was less important than it might seem, because in many states, including Texas, immigrant men exercised these rights without being naturalized. The procedure also granted the protection of the U.S. government to naturalized citizens traveling abroad, among other things shielding them from conscription into foreign armies.[9]

Will underwent the naturalization process on November 22, 1873, in the district court of Jefferson County. In a case listed as "Ex Parte" (on behalf of one person and without an adverse party), he petitioned the presiding judge to "admit him to the rights and privileges of a naturalized citizen of the United States." The judge was William M. Chambers, the same man who had earlier presided over John Leonard's admission to the bar and who was then being castigated by conservative white Democrats for his "scalawag" Republican politics. Petitioning for American citizenship under "the authority of Several Acts of Congress," Will set forth the particulars of his case. He declared that he had emigrated from "the Kingdom of Great Britain," was twenty-one years old, and that for the last three years it had been his "bona fide intention to become a citizen of the United States." He renounced "all allegiance or fidelity to any foreign potentate, state, or sovereignty whatsoever," particularly to "Victoria, Queen of Great Britain."[10]

He took the required oath, pledging allegiance to his new country: "I will support and defend the Constitution and laws of the United States against all enemies, foreign and domestic; that I will bear true faith and allegiance to the same; that I take this obligation freely without any mental reservation or purpose of evasion; So help me God."[11] Judge Chambers, having reviewed Will's petition and heard his oath, admitted him as "a citizen of the United States of America duly naturalized" and ordered the clerk to issue his naturalization papers.[12]

The union of Will and Viola produced prompt and bountiful results. Just eleven months after they married, Viola gave birth to their first child, a daughter named Mittie, born September 19, 1874. Two years later, on October 16, they had a son, Ogden. Four years later, another girl, Alma, was born December 9, 1880. All three of the children enjoyed good health and the care of a loving mother and father, at least during their earliest years.[13] The arrival of his first child changed Will's life, among other things reducing the frequency of his letter writing. About three months after Mittie's birth, he composed a hurried letter to Sarah Ann, apologizing for not having written more often and promising to "write often enough to let you know that I am still alive and in good health." He sent news about Cousin John, or rather commented on the lack of such news: "You must tell Aunt Mary [John's mother] that I have not heard from Coz. Willie [meaning John] lately. When I did, he was in Santa Fe, New Mexico, but he expected to leave there . . . for Arizona or California. . . . It is strange that Aunt Mary has not heard from him, as he told me that he had written several times."[14]

The report concerning his immediate family was favorable and upbeat. "Viola and the baby are both . . . well as usual. I say 'as usual' because Viola has generally got a cold or something, and baby is very fond of having the colic. But really they are in good health." Later in the letter he furnished more comments about the baby. "Tell mother that 'Little Mittie' says 'Goo-Goo' when asked what we shall say to *grandmother*. . . . Although it is only about 3 months old, it is *crowing* already, and can nearly sit alone in any-one's lap."

With the Christmas holidays fast approaching, he employed a seasonal theme to give advice to Sarah Ann, who was romantically involved with a man, identified in the correspondence only as "the Scotchman," and con-templating an engagement. Assuming a worldly tone and at the same time praising the institution of marriage, he counseled, "Christmas or New Year is a good time to join fortunes and promise to trot through the remaining years of this dying life in double harness, with one common yoke."

Will sent his greetings to Sarah Ann for "A Merry Merry Christmas and a Happy New Year," but expressed his regret for not having sent a present. "I am most truly sorry that there is nothing here I can send as a token, but you will accept 'the will for the deed,' and read this letter. . . ." Closing as "Your Affectionate Brother," he signed with a flourish, "*J. W. L. Johnson.*"

During early 1876 Will finally realized his ambition of becoming a lawyer. He obtained his law license in a two-step procedure, first receiving a certificate of qualification from the Jefferson County Commissioner's Court and later passing an oral examination in one of the area district courts. On February 1, 1876, he accomplished the first step, appearing in the Commissioner's Court in Beaumont and submitting his application for a certificate needed "before receiving License as an Attorney." The Court approved his petition, certifying that he had been a citizen of Jefferson County for the last two years, that he was over twenty-one years of age—he was twenty-three—and that he was "a man of good reputation for moral character and honorable deportment."[15]

Within a year of becoming a lawyer, Will found new business opportu-nities for himself. During the spring of 1877, he won a two-year appoint-ment as tax assessor of Jefferson County. Awarded to him by Henry C. Pedigo, judge of the first judicial district, the assessor's position was a part-time job requiring him to inspect all properties in the county, prepare as-sessments, and furnish official rolls to the commissioners court. After submitting the assessment roles to the court, he collected a commission based on the amount of property taxes assessed. His earnings were modest: $85 in 1877 and $109 the next year.[16]

Will probably obtained the assessor's position through both his qualifications and his political connections. His law license plus his teaching and newspaper experience added up to impressive credentials, and he boasted important political friends. Furthermore, his brothers-in-law, Lem and Ed, were well entrenched in courthouse affairs: Ed had served a term as sheriff, and in 1877, when Will got the assessor's job, Lem was holding the position of county treasurer. Indeed, the commission check he received in 1877 was actually issued by Viola's brother.[17]

On October 10, 1877, Will wrote to Sarah Ann, telling her about the assessor's job, mentioning his law practice, and reporting local and family news. The tone of his letter was noticeably sober and mature. Likewise his business letterhead presented a thoroughly professional appearance: "J. W. L. Johnson, Attorney at Law and Land Agent, Beaumont, Texas. Will practice in the Courts of Jefferson, Orange, Liberty, and Hardin Counties." After apologizing for not having answered her last letter and pleading a shortage of time, he explained the particulars of his work as tax assessor:

> Ever since June of this year, until yesterday, I have been very busily engaged attending to my official duties as Assessor of this County. It would take too long to explain this fully to you, but I will say this much; that since June I have had to travel on horseback over the entire County; I have to visit every house, and see that the person assesses his property for taxation at a fair valuation, and make out a list of all the property each person owns. . . . After . . . that, it becomes my duty to make out three copies of all of them.[18]

He told of personal activities, claiming some business progress and noting "I have gained a little practice as an Attorney." He then proceeded to render interesting opinions on economic conditions in Texas. He displayed a mildly pessimistic viewpoint, perhaps reflecting his own financial difficulties and the postwar stagnation and recession from which Beaumont was still suffering: "Times are very hard and dull in Texas, and have been so for two or three years. Fortunes are no longer made in a day here; we have assumed too much the ways and customs of old established countries, and business has been placed on too solid a footing for persons now to jump from comparative poverty to affluence."

He compared the wages and prices in America and England, but was inconclusive about actual differences between the two countries: "It is true that a living may possibly be easier made here than in England, and that living may in many respects be superior to the living of the same class in

England. . . . Wages may seem higher here than in England, but when we take into consideration the relative costs of articles, then they are nearly on the same level." Displaying traditional Victorian attitudes about thrift and hard work, he demonstrated that he understood, at least theoretically, that getting ahead required making and saving money: "One need not come to Texas, or any other Southern state and expect to pick up gold in the street, or pluck it off the trees. . . . A man must work, and work hard and long, if he expects ever to save anything over and above his present expenses."

Turning to more personal matters, he fretted about a minor ailment. "This summer . . . I have been much annoyed with the neuralgia [radiating nerve pains], a complaint prevalent in this country, by reason I suppose, of the great heat." But overall he was pleased with his family's health. "Viola and the children are well and so far, I may say, that we have had unusual good luck." He also provided news about the health of Robert Leonard: "I am sorry to say that Uncle Bob has been seriously afflicted all the summer, the result of, I think, too deep and continuous study. However, he is better now and we entertain great hopes that he will, after a time, surmount his troubles and come out at last." Will's explanation of Uncle Bob's mental condition and its possible causes was less than complete; among other things, he failed to mention that earlier the elder Leonard had suffered a nervous breakdown.[19]

On September 12, 1877, a full month before writing the above letter, Will had initiated a judicial proceeding which would find Robert Leonard legally insane. Acting on behalf of Leonard's wife and children, Will had filed an ex parte application in the Commissioners' Court of Jefferson County. Presented to Judge John C. Milliken, Will's affidavit declared that Robert H. Leonard was "non compos mentis" and "that the welfare of himself and his family required that he should be placed under restraint."[20]

The details of Uncle Bob's illness and his irrational behavior are not known, but legal records reveal that the unfortunate man was brought into court and tried before "a jury of twelve good and lawful men." They included John C. Craig, the Irish-born merchant, and other prominent citizens. First the jury "examined" Leonard in open court and certified various facts about him: a man forty-four years of age, a native of Great Britain, a naturalized citizen of the United States, and a licensed lawyer in Texas. They then declared that Leonard had suffered his insanity for three-and-one-half months, that his condition was not hereditary, that his wife and five children were able to support themselves, but that he did not have the financial means to support himself.[21]

After hearing the evidence, the jury found Leonard "of unsound mind and should be placed under restraint." With this decision, Judge Milliken ordered that he be sent to the State Lunatic Asylum in Austin. In furtherance of this decision, Judge Milliken ordered the county clerk to transmit an application and other papers to the superintendent of the asylum, asking whether there was a vacancy for Robert Leonard.[22]

Apparently a vacancy at the institution was not immediately available, and Uncle Bob was held "under restraint" for two months in Beaumont. Whether he was confined at home or in the county jail is not known, but in either case it was no doubt a distressing situation for the patient and for his family and friends. Will in particular must have suffered during these days, given his close relationship with his uncle, the man who had served as his mentor and role model.

In November 1877, Robert Leonard was transported by the Jefferson County sheriff to the asylum in Austin. The institution, which had opened in 1861, was a state charity hospital that served both public and private patients. "Public" patients, which included Leonard and comprised about ninety percent of its cases, were committed by the court system with expenses paid by state and county funds, while "private" patients were sent by private physicians with fees furnished by family members. Situated on 300 acres just northwest of downtown Austin, the hospital was a handsome limestone structure of large proportions. In 1877 it housed about 230 patients with separate wards for males and females, plus segregated facilities for African American men and women.[23]

At the asylum, Robert Leonard was delivered into the care of the superintendent, Dr. David R. Wallace, a North Carolinian who had received his medical training at New York University. Wallace adhered to popular psychiatric theories on the causes and treatments of mental illness. He believed that insanity was an organic disease, caused by the stresses and complexities of modern society, that the condition was curable, and that the best treatment was a "moral" therapy. The moral treatment involved removal of the patient from a causative environment to heal in orderly and peaceful surroundings. Wallace's regimen included rest, work, and recreation, including frequent walks on the parklike grounds of the asylum. He managed his patients with discipline and kindness, describing his technique as "a hand of iron in a glove of velvet."[24]

When Robert Leonard was admitted, he was among 142 patients, 97 males and 45 females, accepted by Dr. Wallace. The doctor described his patients' insanity in three broad categories: melancholia, dementia, and mania, each with variations of acute and chronic. He also identified some thirty causes of the illnesses, including epilepsy, brain fever, intemperance, solitary habit, religious excitement, and spiritualism. Wallace determined that Robert was suffering from chronic mania, a long-lasting disorder manifested by alternating episodes of excitability and depression, sometimes relieved by periods of normal behavior. He recorded the cause of Robert's mania as "religion and spiritualism," a diagnosis that was repeated later when a newspaper reported that he had "lost his mind" when attending a spiritual seance in Houston.[25]

The spiritualism in which Robert Leonard had involved himself was popular in the United States and England during the Victorian era. Living persons attempted to communicate with the dead through mediums, "professional" spiritualists who organized seances to call forth the spirits of departed ones. While skeptics scoffed at the notion of ghostly seances, numerous prominent citizens, including Queen Victoria and President Lincoln, attended such gatherings. The details of Uncle Bob's involvement in the Houston seance are not known; perhaps he had been trying to communicate with a daughter, Alice Gertrude, who had died three years earlier at the age of twelve.[26]

Apparently Robert responded quickly to Dr. Wallace's treatment. On December 30, 1877, only five weeks after being admitted, he was pronounced "Improved" by Dr. Wallace. Although the doctor did not judge him "Restored," he was discharged from the asylum, and returned to his home in Beaumont. Unfortunately, his mental problems would linger, partially disabling him for at least several years. In the 1880 census, taken during the month of June, he would be counted at his Beaumont residence and listed as a "Lawyer retired," because of "Insanity."[27]

During the period in which Uncle Bob suffered from his mental illness, Will struggled with problems of his own, as he tried to make enough money to meet the needs of his growing family. While working as tax assessor and trying to build his law practice, he returned to the newspaper business. For at least six months during 1877–78, he worked part time as a reporter for John S. Swope, an Iowa native, who published the *Beaumont Lumberman*. Among other topics, he reported news from the local sawmills, covering their rejuvenation after the recent reopening of the railroads.[28]

About the time that Robert Leonard was discharged from the asylum, John returned to Beaumont, probably arriving in January or February of 1878. After an absence of five years, he was drawn back to the city, he said, by the presence of Hannah, "my much beloved sister," who had immigrated to the town during 1875. Whatever business disagreement he had with Uncle Bob was resolved. He moved into the Leonard household on Forsythe Street and quickly took up life as a Beaumonter again. He resumed his law practice and again engaged in local politics; during the fall of 1878 he ran for the position of county attorney and won a two-year term for that office. Later, he would help organize an Episcopal church and also start his own newspaper.[29]

With John's arrival in Beaumont, the members of the Leonard-Johnson-Lamb clan were united in Texas for the first time, numbering eighteen people in all: John, divorced and single; Will, Viola, and their three children; Hannah, Tom, and their four children; and, of course, Uncle Bob, Aunt Rosalie, and their five children. The clan, with Robert Leonard at least its figurehead patriarch, boasted a considerable potential for business and politics. Well educated and widely experienced, they included three practicing attorneys. Except for concerns and embarrassment over Uncle Bob's mental illness, they had every reason to be optimistic about the future.[30]

CHAPTER 7

"HIS HONOR
J. W. L. JOHNSON"

Not long after the Leonard-Johnson-Lamb clan gathered in Beaumont, Will and Viola moved their family to nearby Orange, a town that probably offered him better business opportunities. By June of 1879, he had opened his law office there and was advertising his professional specialties in real estate: "Will render land for assessment, pay taxes, furnish correct abstracts for Jefferson and Orange counties." He also served as a broker, offering "Good farming lands for sale, equal to the best in Southeast Texas."[1]

Twenty-five miles east of Beaumont, Orange was situated on the Texas-Louisiana border. In 1879 the town was very similar to Beaumont, though smaller in population. Its economy was based on farming, ranching, and sawmilling, with steamboats and railroads to carry products to market. Both towns were experiencing a boom in railroad construction and sawmill operations. In June 1879, the *Orange Tribune* printed an enthusiastic report written by William Christian, a Houston businessman, who had just returned from "a flying visit to Orange and Beaumont on the Texas & New Orleans Railroad." In those days, "flying" on the T. & N.O. meant rumbling along at about ten miles per hour, a little faster than a good horse could trot. Christian rendered a glowing report about business prospects in Southeast Texas, declaring Orange and Beaumont as "two of the most flourishing towns of their size in the state."[2]

Christian noted that Orange and Beaumont carried on a considerable trade in cattle and hides but explained that their principal traffic was in lumber and shingles. At Orange there were five lumber and four shingle mills, while in Beaumont there were six mills of each type. According to Christian's calculations, the mills of the two towns together were capable of enormous daily production: 372,000 feet of lumber and 380,000 shingles. The raw materials for the mills were abundant and easily accessible; the supply of pine and cypress timber were described by Christian as "inexhaustible."[3]

Christian was correct in his enthusiasm about the Texas lumber industry and on target in his praise for Orange and Beaumont. During the 1870s and 1880s, the production of lumber ranked as the number one manufacturing industry in Texas, when measured by value added. By 1875, lumber had become the leading industry in tonnage moved annually by the state's railroads. In 1880, Orange and Beaumont, with advantages of raw materials, technology, and transportation, were predominant in the Texas lumber industry, producing at least twenty-eight percent of the state's total output.[4]

Focusing attention on transportation, Christian explained that Orange and Beaumont enjoyed perfect locations, both being situated at the crossroads of steamboat and railroad lines. Orange was located at the highest point of year-round navigation on the Sabine River, while Beaumont occupied a similar position on the Neches. In this way, the towns enjoyed easy steamboat access to Sabine Pass and its steamship connections in the Gulf of Mexico. More important, both towns lay on the route of the Texas & New Orleans Railroad, an ongoing project that would soon connect Houston to New Orleans. During 1876, Orange and Beaumont had been linked to each other and also connected to Houston, so the towns already enjoyed efficient rail transportation for their lumber products to the Houston-Galveston markets. This rail connection to the west helped facilitate dramatic increases in lumber production; between 1870 and 1880 the value of lumber produced in Orange and Jefferson counties soared from $78,000 to $978,400. Christian figured that completion of the T. & N.O. all the way to New Orleans would mean even brighter prospects for Southeast Texas; for Orange and Beaumont, he saw "grand possibilities."[5]

When measured by population growth, Beaumont and Orange were indeed "flourishing" during the late 1870s. Between 1870 and 1880, the number of people in Jefferson County increased from 1906 to 3489, while numbers in Orange County grew from 1255 to 2938. The population of Orange county in 1880 mostly comprised white Southerners engaged in farming and ranching, but about fifteen percent of the total was made up of African Americans, some of whom worked in timber and sawmill operations. Another seventeen percent of the population consisted of non-Southerners and Europeans, most being engaged in railroad construction, lumber operations, and other urban occupations. Among the non-Southerners were Henry J. Lutcher and G. Bedell Moore, both Pennsylvania natives who developed large lumber companies in Orange.[6]

According to the 1880 census, Orange County citizens included twenty-two natives of Great Britain. Among them, only three were engaged in farming or ranching, while the rest pursued urban occupations, many as railroad laborers or sawmill workers. The English Texans included two merchants, a minister, a sawmill owner, and a man who described himself as a "huck-ster." Only two Englishmen qualified as professionals: James Saunders, a forty-three-year-old physician, and Will Johnson, then twenty-seven years old and identified as a lawyer.[7]

In addition to Will, the census listed his wife, Viola, their two young children, Mittie and Ogden, and a servant, Laura Black, a twelve-year-old African American. The employment of a live-in domestic servant probably indicated a certain level of affluence. The census contained an interesting misstatement of Viola's age, listing her as twenty-five when in fact she had already passed her thirty-third birthday. This mistake of eight years likely was made intentionally, either by Will or Viola, perhaps as a joke or maybe out of vanity.[8]

In Orange County, Will capitalized on some of the same political con-nections that had served him in Beaumont. District Judge H. C. Pedigo, who had given him the tax assessor's job in Jefferson County, appointed him to the same position in Orange County. This was actually an elective post, but he was named to the position to replace John Dibert who had re-signed in September. During December, Will posted the necessary surety bond, a $1200 financial guarantee signed by him and three friends, Wilson A. Junker, a "Saloon Proprietor," W. O. Morgan, a farmer, and A. P. Harris, editor and publisher of the *Orange Weekly Tribune*.[9]

To complete his qualification for the assessor's position, Will took the statutory oath, swearing to "faithfully and impartially discharge and per-form all the duties" of the position "to the best of my skill and ability" and in accordance with "the Constitution and laws of the United States and this state." He also swore the oath's anti-dueling provision, declaring that, "since the adoption of the Constitution of this state," he had not "fought a duel with deadly weapons" or "sent or accepted a challenge to fight a duel" or "acted as a second." Thus qualified and sworn, Will became assessor, serving for one year and collecting a modest commission—probably less than $200.[10]

Will practiced law in Orange almost four years. He officed by himself but sometimes worked as co-counsel with other Orange County lawyers, such as John T. Hart, an Alabama native. Like Will and Viola, John Hart and his wife, Addie, were young, and also just starting their family. The Harts and the Johnsons may have socialized together, sharing the experiences of prac-ticing law and rearing children. Will and John became members of the Orange Rifles, a volunteer militia group that included a number of the town's leading citizens. While primarily serving law enforcement purposes, Orange

Rifle members also enjoyed social and civic benefits. During holiday festivals, they marched in parades, wearing uniforms, and carrying banners.[11]

Will joined other civic organizations, further establishing himself in the town. He became a member of the Orange Knights of Honor, a benevolent and mutual life insurance association, and the East Texas and West Louisiana River and Harbor Improvement Association, a group dedicated to the development of the Sabine waterway—the pass, the lake, and the river. The waterway association proposed to solicit the cooperation of Beaumont and other communities and to lobby Congress for dredging appropriations. Will was elected assistant secretary of this organization and was also chosen to serve on the executive committee.[12]

Practicing law in Orange County, Will came in contact with other local attorneys, including John T. Stark, an Ohio native who had served in the Confederate army, and Stephen Chenault, a Tennessean who was related by marriage to George W. O'Brien. O'Brien, the Beaumont attorney for whom Will had worked in the newspaper business, was married to Chenault's sister, Ellen. Sometimes Chenault and O'Brien practiced law together, advertising themselves as a partnership and listing offices in Orange and Beaumont. With the two towns so conveniently connected by railroad, O'Brien and other Beaumont attorneys frequently worked cases in the Orange District Court.[13]

Will was involved in a variety of Orange County cases, both civil and criminal. His civil cases included actions for debt collection, garnishment enforcement, and land partition. He represented Wilson Junker in two cases involving business debt, one when Junker was a plaintiff and the other, a defendant. Junker, the saloon keeper who had signed as a surety for Will, also needed legal representation in various criminal matters. During 1879, he was charged at least five times with minor offenses such as "Allowing gaming in his house" and "Violation of the Sunday law." The records do not show what lawyer represented Junker in these criminal cases, but probably it was Will Johnson.[14]

He handled a number of divorce cases, such as the one in which Julie Blair sued Daniel Blair. In January 1881, Will wrote out the court papers in his own hand, accusing Daniel Blair of "cruel treatment," being "drunk from use of intoxicating liquors," and threatening "to kill the plaintiff." He also fashioned long interrogatories that were sent to Fannin County, where the couple had lived previously and where the defendant resided currently. In October of that year, the district judge ruled in favor of Will's client, granting the divorce to Julie Blair and awarding her custody of their son.[15]

In another divorce case, Will represented Helen Patton in her suit against Robert Patton. According to the petition that Will composed, Mr. Patton had disappeared, and Mrs. Patton asked for divorce on grounds of abandonment. She alleged that she had been "a kind and affectionate wife," but that he had left her "without any just cause" and "without providing for her comfort and welfare." These charges that Will drafted against Robert Patton were very similar to the ones that later would be lodged against him by Viola.[16]

Will worked on a number of serious criminal cases in Orange County, including one in which he defended Sandy Smith, a man accused of robbery and assault to commit murder. During October 1879, Will defended Smith in a jury trial, but the verdict went against them. Smith was found guilty of both charges and sentenced to prison for consecutive terms of two and seven years. Another criminal case involved H. McDowell, a saloon keeper and faro dealer charged in October 1879 with the murder of one John Hoge. According to a witness, McDowell had killed Hoge by hitting him over the head with "a tolerable heavy chair." During May of the next year, McDowell was tried before a jury and acquitted. It is not known whether Will was involved in McDowell's defense, but there was some connection between the two; later McDowell would be called as a defense witness when Will himself was faced with criminal charges.[17]

In another case, one that attracted considerable attention in Orange and Jefferson Counties, Will helped handle the defense of James D. Bullock, a former sheriff of Jefferson County. Bullock had been charged with multiple counts of malfeasance in office, including embezzlement, forgery, perjury, and misapplication of public money. First indicted in Jefferson County in 1877, Bullock had been granted a change of venue to Orange County in 1879. There, he hired three defense attorneys: Will Johnson, John Stark, and John Leonard, who traveled from Beaumont to help with the case. John, who had known Bullock earlier and once roomed in his house, described the defendant as "a slippery character."[18]

As Bullock's cases proceeded through the court, he remained free on surety bonds, his future court appearances guaranteed by the financial deposits provided by several local citizens, including Lem Ogden, Will's brother-in-law. The nature of Lem Ogden's relationship to Bullock is not known, but records show that Ogden and the others forfeited their surety deposits when Bullock failed to make one of his scheduled court appearances. Will, John, and Mr. Stark shepherded the Bullock cases through various legal procedures but were never forced to defend them in a trial.

Bullock died during 1879 and his cases were abated. Later, Lem Ogden and the other sureties apparently recovered their deposits.[19]

By the spring of 1880, Will had proved himself as "a lawful lawyer" in Orange County. The court records contain various references to him and his cases, though not as many as those relating to some of his fellow lawyers, such as Hart, Stark, and Chenault. Whether he was earning enough money to support his family is not known, but, overall, the future must have looked bright. On April 12, he attended the opening session of the spring term of the district court and participated in attendant rituals. On that day, the presiding judge, H. C. Pedigo, had not arrived, and, as was traditional, the lawyers in attendance conducted an election among themselves to determine who would take the bench on a temporary basis. "J. W. L. Johnson, Esq." and "J. T. Stark, Esq." were among those who received votes, with Johnson being elected and enjoying the honor of serving as presiding judge. The next day, when Will surrendered the bench to Judge Pedigo, his service and name were recorded in the court minutes: "His Honor J. W. L. Johnson."[20]

CHAPTER 8

"I Know Them 'Piscopals"

John Leonard and Will Johnson had been reared as Anglicans, but when they moved to Beaumont they did not find a church of their faith. The Episcopal Church, known formally as the Protestant Episcopal Church of the United States and derived directly from the Church of England, had not been organized in Southeast Texas; and there were few people in the area identified as Anglicans or Episcopalians.

John learned about the scarcity of Anglicans during 1870, when he moved to the nearby village of Hardin to practice law. One day he stopped to visit with a group of local men who had gathered on the porch of Captain Parker's general store.

> One of them asked John: "You're a Methodist ain't ye, Squire?"
> "No," he said.
> "There," said another, "I told ye he was a Baptist."
> He shook his head.
> "What are ye then?"
> "Episcopalian," John replied.
> Most of the men were ignorant of such a church, but one of them said, "O'yes, I know them 'Piscopals. They uster have 'em in Georgy. Minister wears a nightshirt to preach in."[1]

John's story may be apocryphal but it provides an accurate picture of the religious situation in Southeast Texas at the time; Methodists and Baptists were numerous and well organized, while Jews, Catholics, Episcopalians, and others were few in number and had not yet coalesced into viable congregations.

John remembered that the people of Hardin County held conservative religious views: "The country immediately around Hardin . . . was a dense forest of yellow pine trees, some of the tallest and finest in the land. . . . The people, like the physical surroundings, were devoid of artificiality. They lived plain and . . . decent lives, chiefly of the rural cast. For the most part, they were neighborly and there were few clashes of opinion, except on one subject: religion."[2]

The Hardin people were "sincerely religious," he recalled. "They belonged almost unanimously to the Methodist or Baptist denominations, and each held very narrow views about dancing and other amusements." On one occasion John attended a local party and observed some young people who dared to dance a Virginia reel. They danced wildly, swinging their partners and clicking their heels. Later he heard that eight of the dancers had lost their church memberships, having "danced themselves outen the church."[3]

Group religious practice in Southeast Texas mostly was evangelical in nature and often featured "protracted meetings," or revival camp meetings. John witnessed such gatherings at Sour Lake, a Hardin County hamlet, and at Hardin and Beaumont. Featuring the appearance of circuit riding pastors, the protracted meetings were frequently held indoors at the local courthouse. "At old Hardin," he explained, "when a preacher was expected, written notices would be put up on the door . . . of the courthouse stating that 'God willing, a protracted meeting will be held in the courtroom next Tuesday evening at candlelighting.'"[4]

"The first meeting's attendance depended on the spread of the notice," John recalled. "If those who came liked the preacher, the crowd would increase and the meeting might run on four or five days. . . . Few of the preachers were strong on theology, but they knew their Bible and preached the word as they understood it, with fervor."[5]

One such traveling preacher was Father Woollam, a spirited old Methodist whose preaching John heard in a protracted meeting at the county courthouse in Beaumont. Reverend John Pipkin, the resident Methodist minister, opened the services with "a good sermon of sound doctrine and evangelistic fervor." Then, Father Woollam took center stage and delivered an emotional address, recounting the recent discovery of a photograph of his long-dead mother. "It was very pathetic and a masterpiece of appeal," John recollected. "As the sermon reached its climax, several persons came forward and professed conversion." With a somewhat jaundiced eye, John remarked that on at least two subsequent occasions, he saw Father Woollam employ the same tear-jerking tactic, calling forth the image of his mother and producing the same telling effect.[6]

As in Hardin County, Beaumont and Jefferson County were dominated by Methodists and Baptists. John recalled that these two groups had no churches of their own but conducted regular Sunday services in the courthouse. And there was no full-time preacher in the town, other than "Parson" Pipkin, who operated a local sawmill: "The only resident clergyman of that time was Rev. John F. Pipkin, a Methodist, whose Christian faith was firm, a sound preacher and a minister whose service to the people of Beaumont was not guided by denominational fetters, but extended to all who needed wise counsel or humane help in sorrow, sickness or death, and who served at baptisms, marriages or funerals as the general ministrant of Beaumont."[7]

As for Anglicans, a local church history claims that Will Johnson and John Leonard were "the first Episcopalians to live in Beaumont." But this seems unlikely, considering that a number of Englishmen had lived in Beaumont before the Civil War and likely at least some of them had been reared in the Anglican Church and would have qualified as Episcopalians. Nevertheless, the number of local Episcopalians was certainly small, and the denomination was not well-known in Southeast Texas.[8]

The Episcopal Church was well established in other parts of Texas. Numerous congregations had been organized before the Civil War, including the earliest three: Christ Church in Matagorda and Christ Church in Houston, both founded in 1839, and Trinity Church, established in Galveston in 1841. By 1859, when Reverend Alexander Gregg was elected to serve as the first bishop of the Episcopal diocese of Texas, the church boasted more than twenty parishes, including churches in San Augustine, Nacogdoches, Austin, San Antonio, and Brownsville.[9]

Alexander Gregg served as the bishop of Texas for thirty-three years and during this time placed his mark indelibly upon the diocese of Texas. He steered the church through the tumultuous times of secession, war, emancipation, and Reconstruction. He labored to spread the faith to cities and towns throughout Texas, including Beaumont, where he influenced the lives of John Leonard and other Southeast Texans. Bishop Gregg was a genuine Southerner. Born and reared in a slaveholding South Carolina family, he attended college and practiced law before becoming rector of Saint David's parish in his hometown of Cheraw. Accepting the call to the episcopacy of Texas, he moved his family to Austin in 1860. There, he set up a household that included his wife, seven children and twenty-six slaves. How he employed and cared for his slaves is not known, but it is clear that he was committed to the institution of slavery and the Southern way of life.[10]

On the questions of slavery, secession, and war, Bishop Gregg and the Texas diocese followed the same path as Anglican dioceses in the other Southern states. The national Episcopal Church, unlike the Baptists, Methodists, and Presbyterians, had not divided itself earlier into Northern

and Southern branches over the slavery question. It was only the act of secession that precipitated a sectional rupture among the Episcopalians; for
them, it was primarily a matter of nationality, not unlike when the American
church arose out of the Colonies' separation from England. When the
Southern states officially seceded from the Union, the Southern dioceses,
including Texas, withdrew from the national church and established the
Protestant Episcopal Church of the Confederate States of America. Bishop
Gregg favored secession and supported the Confederate cause. During the
war, he would suffer the tragic loss of his son Alexander, Jr., who died of
pneumonia while serving in the Confederate army.[11]

When the South was defeated and reunited with the Union, the
Southern dioceses again followed the principle of nationality, disbanding
their sectional organization and rejoining the national church. Bishop
Gregg quickly adapted to the political realities and facilitated rapid reconciliation of the Texas diocese with the Northern churches; he sent deputies
to the General Convention in Philadelphia in 1865 and the same year took
an oath of loyalty to the Union.[12]

During Reconstruction and the subsequent postwar years, Bishop Gregg
worked to expand and develop the church in Texas. The field was rich with
potential members; the state's white population was growing rapidly, from
420,000 in 1860 to 565,000 in 1870, and to 1,200,000 in 1880. But competition among the denominations for members was intense, especially with the
Methodist and Baptist Churches, the state's two largest antebellum denominations, which continued to grow after the war.[13]

In 1870 the Methodists recorded 34,772 white members with 355 congregations and 244 buildings, while the Baptists, who did not count members,
had 275 congregations and 211 church buildings. Other religious groups, such
as the Presbyterians, Roman Catholics, and Episcopalians, were much smaller
in terms of membership. The Texas Episcopal diocese in 1870 reported
only 1700 communicants with 32 congregations and 31 edifices. In terms of
sheer numbers, then, the Episcopalians were of minor consequence.[14]

The Episcopal Church did not appeal to most Texans. Southern whites
apparently were not attracted by the formal liturgical worship required of
Anglicans. Only a relatively few preferred what Bishop Gregg called the
"system of the church," the annual schedule of orderly worship and the
strict adherence to the Book of Common Prayer. But for some European
immigrants, the Anglican tradition—with its ancient prayer book, traditional rituals, and robed clergymen—provided needed reminders of the
Old World religious and social order they left behind. For others, particu-

larly those who wanted quiet and dignified forms of worship, the church
furnished a welcome haven from the more emotional and enthusiastic pre-
sentations of Christianity that were so common on the Texas frontier.[15]

If the Episcopalians were few in number, their congregations often included a disproportionate number of prominent and influential citizens. In
Galveston, Houston, and Austin, the three largest Anglican congregations,
the memberships included many notable businessmen and city leaders.
Among the congregants at Houston's Christ Church, for example, were
railroad developer W. J. Hutchins, wholesale merchant Thomas W.
House, and financier and philanthropist William Marsh Rice.[16]

Bishop Gregg carried out strenuous missionary activities, traveling
about the state, baptizing children, performing marriages, conducting services, and founding new congregations. Sometimes he traveled alone, other
times with assistants such as Reverend Edwin Wickens, an English native
who served many years as archdeacon of the diocese.[17]

In 1876 the bishop paid official calls to Beaumont, Sabine Pass, and
Hardin—towns which, he said, "had never before been visited by a
Clergyman of the Church." The next year he returned to Southeast Texas,
this time to Orange, where he found "a goodly band of communicants . . .
anxious to forward the establishment of the Church." Seeds of a congregation had already been planted in Orange. During the war, Reverend J.
Wood Dunn, an Episcopal rector from Louisiana, had sojourned in the
town and conducted services there. In 1878, Bishop Gregg traveled again to
Orange, this time accompanied by Reverend Wickens; together they performed baptisms and confirmations and administered holy communion.[18]

While Bishop Gregg and Reverend Wickens worked to build their congregation in Orange, they likely cast a prospecting eye at Beaumont.
Situated just twenty miles to the west, Beaumont was enjoying the redevel-
opment and expansion of the railroads and sawmills. In 1876 the railroad to
Houston had been reopened, and by 1880 the sawmills in Beaumont were
booming with the production of export lumber. With the railroads and
sawmills came a healthy influx of new people. By the late 1870s, the population of Beaumont had grown to almost 2000, nearly double that at the beginning of the decade. Among the newcomers were many non-Southerners
and white collar workers, groups that included prospective members for
the Episcopalians.[19]

The prospective Anglicans included John Leonard, who had returned
to Beaumont in 1878, and his sister, Hannah Lamb, and her family. Also,
there was Hannah's friend Joanna Curtis, whom John credited as the prime

instigator of the Beaumont Episcopal Church. Born in Pennsylvania, Joanna had recently moved to town with her husband, Lorenzo B. Curtis, a lumberyard clerk who hailed from New York. She and her husband had no children of their own, but their household included her four sons by a previous marriage. When not keeping house, Joanna was often engaged in local charitable activities.[20]

One day in 1879, while John was visiting in her residence, she told him about a destitute Catholic woman whose husband had just died, and she lamented the lack of a local priest to conduct the funeral. John sympathized and then casually expressed a wish that they had an Episcopal Church in the town. To this, Joanna responded with a phrase proudly recorded in local Anglican history: "What's the use of wishing?" and added, "let's start one."[21]

Then and there, with Joanna looking over his shoulder, John sat down and wrote a letter to Bishop Gregg, asking "how we could organize the nucleus of a church." With that step taken, Joanna undertook a survey of the town, looking for Anglicans and other prospective members. The next week, having received a favorable reply to their inquiry from Reverend Wickens, they convened a small group in John's law offices, where he drafted a formal application to Reverend Wickens asking him to come to Beaumont and assist them with the initial steps. All in attendance signed the application: John, Joanna, Hannah, William Monroe, a divorced sawmill bookkeeper who hailed from Canada, and the Bacon sisters, Julia and Kate, schoolteachers born in Georgia. So the first group was few in numbers but diverse in origins: two English, two Georgians, one New Yorker, and one Canadian.[22]

Soon, sometime during late 1879, Mr. Wickens came to Beaumont and in the Temperance Hall conducted "the first Episcopal service ever held in Beaumont." He also helped John and the others arrange weekly services, organize a Sunday school, and initiate a confirmation class. Wickens christened the new congregation "The Mission of the Good Shepherd."[23]

Early the next year, Bishop Gregg, then making his spring visitation to Southeast Texas, traveled to Beaumont. Services were held in the Union Church, a structure owned jointly by the Methodists and Baptists and described by John as "neat but none too large." There, on January 19, 1880, Bishop Gregg officially organized the Beaumont church and installed John as lay reader-in-charge. The Bishop confirmed several new members, including John and a Mrs. Jamie H. Cleveland. According to John, they had a full house for the services. "To many who attended. . . . it was the first sight of a preacher in robes. But all who came admitted that the sermon was wonderful."[24]

On the fifth Sunday of February 1880, Reverend Wickens returned to

Beaumont, referring to it as "this important mission." He noted happily that "not withstanding the very inclement weather, large congregations attended the services morning and evening," and that "the Holy Communion was celebrated."[25]

Favorably impressed, Reverend Wickens described Beaumont as "quite a flourishing town—our church element is larger than usually found in interior towns, our members are united and very earnest, and in a short time we trust to hear of the laying of the corner stone of their new church." His comment comparing Beaumont to "interior towns" probably referred to the demographic and occupational diversity of the town, as contrasted with other East Texas towns populated almost entirely by Methodists and Baptists who had come to Texas from the Lower South.[26]

Early members of the Mission of the Good Shepherd were indeed diverse in origins. In addition to John, Hannah and Tom Lamb, Joanna and Lorenzo Curtis, and the others already mentioned, the congregation included Louis Miller, bookkeeper from Louisiana; John C. Craig, merchant from Ireland; Colonel B. D. Crary, railroad contractor from New York; and Harvey Wakefield, sawmill lawyer from Pennsylvania. While the group was diverse in origins, it exhibited a white-collar commonality in occupations: clerks, teachers, a newspaperman, accountant, lawyer, and merchant.[27]

Two people close to John who did not appear as members of the Episcopal congregation were Will and Uncle Bob. Will, who had been reared as an Anglican, was nevertheless not recorded in the Beaumont church records or mentioned by John as a member of the local congregation. Of course, during the years 1879–81, when John and the others were organizing the Beaumont church, Will and his wife and family lived in Orange.[28] Uncle Bob probably had been reared as an Anglican but in Texas he became a devoted Methodist. During the years when John was starting the Episcopal congregation, Uncle Bob was plagued by mental illness. Despite this disability, he remained an active member of the local Methodist congregation. He gave generously to the Methodist building fund and aspired to lay leadership in the congregation. In church records he was identified variously as "Brother Leonard" and "Reverend R. H. Leonard."[29]

During its infancy, the Mission of the Good Shepherd did not have a full-time minister and was served by a number of visiting and interim clergymen. Among them were Reverend Wickens, Mr. Dunn from Orange, Stephen G. Burton from Belton, and J. C. Waddill from Matagorda. For much of this period, John acted as the leader of the congregation. He had received his official lay reader's license on March 9, 1880, and in addition to reading services he served as administrative manager of the congregation. Employing the same skills of writing and speaking that served him as teacher and lawyer, John conducted services and handled correspondence with the Bishop's office.[30]

In April 1881, soon after John helped organize the Beaumont church, he was invited to be an official delegate to the annual Diocesan Council in Palestine, Texas. Already acquainted with Bishop Gregg and Reverend Wickens, John found ready acceptance among the twenty priests and fourteen laymen that composed the delegation. The laymen were a varied group, with members hailing originally from South Carolina, Virginia, Maryland, New York, Ireland, and England. The lay delegates included a large number of business and professional people, including a physician, five lawyers, and two wealthy Houston businessmen: W. J. Hutchins, the New York-born railroad developer, and Benjamin A. Botts, the Virginia-born president of City Bank.[31]

During these years the Texas Episcopal Church had a strong English flavor, and this may partially explain why John was so readily accepted. English accents were common in the pulpits, and English natives were prominent in the governing councils. Bishop Gregg was a South Carolinian, but a surprising number of his leading clergymen were English. Among the twenty rectors attending the Diocesan Council, five were English-born. Edwin Wickens, the archdeacon, was an Englishman as were Reverends Julyan J. Clemens, Thomas B. Lee, George W. Dumbell, and Horatio C. Howard. Clemens and Lee, both dynamic and notable figures, headed the important congregations at Houston and Austin respectively, while Dumbell served as host to the Diocesan Council at his church in Palestine. At the opening session of the council, Englishmen played leading roles; Reverend Clemens offered the official opening prayers, and Reverend Wickens preached the council sermon.[32]

At Palestine, John was elected a trustee for the University of the South at Sewanee, Tennessee. This was a significant compliment, because the university, patterned after Oxford, was a revered church institution and a pet project of Bishop Gregg, one of its founders. Unfortunately, John never served as a university trustee, later explaining that he was unable, "as my health failed."[33] Perhaps more importantly, John was appointed by Bishop Gregg to serve with two clergymen, Stephen M. Bird and J. J. Page, on a special council committee dealing with questions pertaining to African Americans. The committee was asked to make recommendations about the means by which "this Church can be brought into more active religious relationship to that interesting class of our people, the colored population of this Diocese."[34]

Here, John and the two priests had to deal with ongoing racial questions that nagged all of Texas society, questions concerning public education, politics, and religion: how should society adjust to accommodate the freedmen? More specifically, how should Episcopalians serve the spiritual needs of the freedmen? Should the African Americans be offered full membership in the church and could they be persuaded to join the congregations? As a slaveowner, Bishop Gregg had tried to minister to the blacks, preaching to them and baptizing their children. Now he followed the same course, urging his white congregations to make room in their churches for the freedmen and to provide schools for them.[35]

The questions pertaining to African Americans were not unique to Texas. Throughout the South, Episcopalians struggled with the issue of how to deal with the freedmen. Before the war, slaveholding had been common among Episcopalians, and the denomination included many of the largest slaveholders, particularly in Virginia and South Carolina. In many cases, as with Bishop Gregg, the Episcopalians had provided for the spiritual needs of the slaves, arranging for their marriages and baptisms, and sometimes even granting them church membership, although of a second-class, segregated variety. Many slaves thus had been associated closely with the Episcopal Church. After emancipation, many Southern white congregations reached out to the freedmen and offered them membership, but it was a limited membership, with no admission to full church fellowship and no hope of ordination of black ministers.[36]

On the last day of the Palestine council, John, Reverend Bird, and Reverend Page offered their report with regard "to the colored people in this Diocese." Reverend Bird introduced their resolution proclaiming that the position taken by the Texas church in 1867 was still valid and that the report of that year dealing with "the religious interests of the freedmen" should be reaffirmed.[37] Accordingly, the council officially adopted the "Report of the Committee upon the Moral and Spiritual Condition and Wants of the Freedmen." Claiming an earnest desire to serve the African Americans but conceding frustration and failure, the Episcopalians concluded that "the main problem" was "how to reach them."[38]

Here, the church inadvertently revealed its longstanding attitudes of prejudice and paternalism. Admitting its "weighty responsibility" to minister to the moral and spiritual wants of the freedmen, it pleaded that "difficulties . . . of a grave and insurmountable character meet us at every step."[39]

They prefer . . . preachers of their own color, which we cannot supply them, and . . . decline all our offers to preach to them. Like all illiterate people, . . . they are ever prone to indulge in feelings of suspicion and
distrust at every offer we make to help them; and . . . worst of all, their
hereditary and constitutional bias, in favor of the most extravagant and
superstitious views in religion, inclines them to prefer extempore forms
of worship to the calm, dignified and orderly service of our Liturgy, and
hence they have generally . . . preferred the ministrations of their colored
brethren, unrestrained by any written forms, as allowing more latitude
for the exercise of their superstitious fancies.[40]

By 1881, when John and the Episcopalians debated the freedmen question, the answer had already been given by the black people themselves. In
Texas and all across the South, the African Americans withdrew en masse
from white congregations and formed churches of their own, black congregations with black ministers, mostly of the Baptist and Methodist denominations. In Beaumont, the freedmen organized the Saint Paul African
Methodist Episcopal Church. There, the new church thrived; they acquired their own church building and met weekly, with Sunday school in
the morning and full services in the afternoon.[41]

Soon after John, Joanna Curtis, and the other local Anglicans established
their Good Shepherd mission, they began efforts to erect a church building.
In March 1881, they purchased a pair of lots on the corner of Forsythe and
Orleans Streets, only two blocks from John's office, and commenced fund
raising efforts. Again, John and Joanna provided the leadership. She persuaded him to organize a dramatic company to earn money for the project.
As a youth, he had been attached for a time to a touring company in England and from this experience had come to love the theater and the lime-
light. With Joanna's help, he assembled the Beaumont Amateurs and was
soon producing light comedies from the Victorian stage.[42]

On May 21, 1881, the Beaumont Amateurs took out an advertisement in
the *Beaumont Enterprise,* which John had recently founded. According to
the announcement, they would stage a double bill on the following Saturday evening. The first production would be *Poor Pillicoddy,* billed as "a
laughable farce," while the second would be *A Quiet Family,* "a screaming
farce." The plays would be staged at Blanchette Opera House at 8:00 P.M.,
with admission of 50 cents and proceeds "applied to the building fund of
the Episcopal church."[43]

John directed both productions and played leading roles, along with

Hannah and Tom Lamb and, of course, Joanna Curtis. Hannah and Tom, who had been married in Anglican Cathedral in Calcutta, became devoted and prominent members of the Beaumont church. Both were musically talented; she played the piano for church services and they sang together in the choir.[44]

Under Joanna's inspiration and John's leadership, the Beaumont Amateurs fared well. Recalling that the plays "took well and offended nobody," he noted their growing success: "We became more ambitious and staged Broughman's extravaganza [*Pocahontas*] with Miss Betty Jackson of Orange in the title role. Mr. Lamb as John Smith and Mrs. Lamb in another part added to the attractiveness by their songs, for both had beautiful voices. I was Powhatan. We played this production to the unprecedented run of three nights, and later took it to Orange for a performance there."[45]

Their fund raising produced quick results, and soon the congregation had funds enough to construct its first church. It was a small frame building, neat and trim, unadorned except for a simple wooden cross that surmounted its peaked roof. The interior was likewise modest in proportions and appearance, with a low flat ceiling, rectangular windows to each side and a gothic opening at the front over the altar. Planked floors were furnished with rows of wooden chairs and the carpeted dais featured a spinet piano and a podium that was lighted by an ornate oil lamp suspended from the ceiling.[46]

Construction of a church building prompted the Episcopalians to convert their mission to a parish, a step that provoked a brief squabble among its members. At a meeting of the vestry, John and other vestrymen took up the question of a permanent name for the new parish. At the request of Reverend Wickens, who originally had named the mission, John put forth the suggestion of Good Shepherd. Louis Miller and Colonel Crary objected, thinking the name was "too suggestive of salvation and soup for down and outers in the slums." As an alternative John suggested the name of one of the evangelists, perhaps Luke. Mr. Miller argued that Saint Luke had come to connote a hospital and as an alternative put forth the name of Saint Mark, a suggestion that drew unanimous approval. On this happy note, John and the other Beaumont Episcopalians completed the inauguration of their church and gave life to an institution that thrives today.[47]

CHAPTER 9

"A POOR THING, SIR—
BUT MINE OWN"

In earlier years, Beaumont had seen several short-lived newspapers, the most recent being the *Beaumont Lumberman,* published during 1876–80 by John S. Swope. This was the paper where Will had worked part time in 1877–78. In 1880 Swope gave up his paper and moved to Houston, leaving the town without a public voice and abandoning the old printing plant that he had been buying on time from George W. O'Brien. John Leonard remembered the *Lumberman* as "badly printed" and recalled that its demise was "unwept, unhonored and unsung."[1]

Beaumont needed a newspaper and several local businessmen, including the merchant John C. Craig, approached John to take up the task. Craig was aware of his previous journalistic experience, including his recent stint as editor of a paper in Prescott, Arizona. John demurred, but Craig persisted, arguing that he was "the logical man to start the paper that was much needed" and that he was "the only man in town hankering for newspaper life." John finally agreed to the proposition, confessing that he had indeed been bitten by the "newspaper bug" and was afflicted with "the itch for scribbling."[2]

John's inclination for the journalism business is not surprising, given the overall popularity of newspapers among English Victorians. A number of the Englishmen who immigrated to Texas, including John and Will, became professional journalists, and some rose to leadership positions in the newspaper business. Manxman D. Richardson, who had moved to Texas in 1852, worked for the *Galveston News* and subsequently helped establish the widely respected *Texas Almanac;* George B. Dealey, who came to the Lone Star State soon after Will and John, also worked for the *Galveston News* and later created the *Dallas Morning News;* and in later years, Henry Hutchings started two Austin papers, the *Evening News* and the *Statesman.*[3]

John's aptitude for the newspaper profession was an outgrowth of his British school education and his facility with the English language. The same language skills that had served him as teacher and lawyer worked well for him as a newspaperman. He wrote clearly and coherently, although he often published his journalistic writings hurriedly, without careful editing and polishing.

John purchased O'Brien's printing outfit, describing it as "the *Lumberman* wreckage" and remembering "the old Washington hand press" as "the most useful item." O'Brien took two mortgage notes, one payable in seven months and the other in fourteen. As John readied his plant for operation, people in town began suggesting names for the new paper. Some recommended the titles of hometown papers in Mississippi and Georgia, while others liked "zoological ones," such as the "Bee" or the "Rattler." John opted for the "Enterprise," the name of the paper he had edited in Arizona.[4]

To start operations, John hired two employees. One was John W. Thackara, a Florida native who had worked for Swope on the *Lumberman.* Thackara was remembered as "an indifferent printer" but "a fairly speedy compositor" and a valuable hand, because he knew how to operate the Washington press. The other was a sixteen-year-old whose name has been lost to history but was described as "a chubby boy" who had served as a printer's devil with a newspaper in Meridian, Mississippi. The youngster was "willing and strong, and could use the composing stick."[5]

Putting out the first issue on a timely basis proved a difficult task. John worked side-by-side with his two employees, struggling to complete the paper on Saturday, November 6, 1880, the date printed on the masthead. By nine that evening, they were still "a column or two shy" and the pages had been printed on one side only. Hampered by "miserable lighting conditions," John sent his workers home, ordering them to come back "bright and early in the morning."[6]

On Sunday morning they returned to the job and worked as rapidly as they could. Soon all the type was set, except for a gap of five lines on page three. John ordered the devil to fill the space and the youngster asked what he wanted. "Five lines," John shouted impatiently, "and make it snappy." In a few minutes the young man filled the blanks and proceeded with the actual printing, tightening the groins and making the very first copy. As the paper came out of the machine, John looked to see what the youngster had set. "The new devil set this up," the boy announced to everyone, "and if you don't like my typesetting, you can get someone else—and don't you forget it."[7]

When John released the first edition of the *Enterprise* on that Sunday, a few citizens chided him for having violated the Sabbath, but he defended himself with "an ox-in-the-ditch sort of plea." Overall the paper was well received and local reactions were described as "generous." John prided himself on his new creation: "A poor thing, sir—but mine own."[8]

John launched his new paper with a "Salutatory" column, promising his readers to make "the *Enterprise* the true representative of Jefferson County and South East Texas." He vowed to cover "all the news of the town and to make local affairs a specialty." In terms of business news, he pledged to cover the lumber industry, giving it "the prominence its importance deserves," at the same time devoting ample attention to the interests of farmers and stockmen. Politically, he declared simply "We are Democratic." But editorially he promised a "free, fair and independent spirit," one that would "not be afraid to speak out . . . against anything we deem to be wrong or unjust."9

John had plenty of political news for the first issue of his paper. In an article titled "It Is All Over—Garfield Elected with a Republican Congress," he recounted the latest returns from the general elections and outlined the continuing dominance of the national government by Republicans. James A. Garfield, the Republican congressman from Ohio, won the presidential election, defeating Winfield S. Hancock, the Civil War general who had served as the Democratic standard bearer, and James B. Weaver, the Greenback Party candidate.10

John ascribed the national Republican victory to a variety of factors, including plentiful harvests, general prosperity, and "the monied people of the north . . . [who] dreaded change, threw their influence to the republican candidates and launched out their money lavishly to secure success." With some disdain he explained to his readers that the campaign had been run to a large extent on the "bloody shirt" issue, with Republicans blaming Democrats for having started the recent war. Because of the election results, he was "sorely disappointed" but reconciled to the situation, so long as the Republicans did not return to the corrupt practices of the Grant administration.11

Although Garfield was elected president, he did not carry Texas. The Democrat Hancock won the state by a wide margin, garnering 156,000 votes as opposed to 57,000 for Garfield and 27,000 for Weaver. The Democrats likewise were victorious in the state races. Oran M. Roberts, the former secessionist leader and Confederate veteran, was easily re-elected governor, polling 166,000 to 64,000 for Edmund J. Davis, the former Republican governor, and 34,000 for William H. Hamman, the Greenback candidate. Texas thus remained firmly in the hands of the conservative white Democrats, even though the Republican Party with its large contingent of African American voters continued to turn out in significant numbers.12

In Jefferson County, Governor Roberts captured the most votes, but the Republican Davis demonstrated surprising strength. He attracted 184 votes against 237 for Roberts, with no votes recorded for the Greenback candidate. The strong showing by the Republicans probably was the result of a relatively large turnout by African American voters. The black population had increased significantly in Jefferson County, growing from twenty-seven percent of the total in 1870 to thirty-four percent in 1880. In all likelihood they were drawn to the area by employment opportunities in lumber; of the African American men who lived and worked in Beaumont, more than seventy percent were employed in that industry. Most performed manual labor, but some had earned skilled positions as carpenters and sawmill foremen.[13]

Aside from the growth of the African American population, the demographic composition of Jefferson County remained fairly constant compared to that of 1870. The proportion of non-Southerners—persons born in European countries and northern states—continued steady at about seven percent. Largely populated by natives of Southern states, Jefferson County's population was in that respect quite similar to other East Texas counties and to the Lower South in general. The contingent of English Americans had increased slightly, however, rising in real numbers from 19 in 1870 to 26 in 1880. Three of the English Texans engaged in agricultural pursuits, while the others followed a variety of urban occupations related to sawmills, railroads, steamboats, and retail. The most prominent white collar English were Uncle Bob, Tom and Hannah Lamb, and of course John Leonard.[14]

As noted earlier, the total population of Jefferson County in 1880 amounted to 3,439. Beaumont counted 1,670 people, but with surrounding precincts could claim a total population of 2,973. It was a viable little town, with railroads, sawmills, stores, hotels, and saloons; but it was very small when compared to Galveston with 22,248 people and Houston with 16,513. John no doubt conceded that Beaumont was not in the same league as these cities, but he did claim a dominant position for his town in the East Texas region. "Beaumont is now and must continue to be the largest and most important town in Eastern Texas," he declared, reluctantly excepting "Marshall, perhaps." Indeed, Marshall had a population of 7,207.[15]

John also was certain that Beaumont was superior to Orange, the nearby town where Will lived and where A. P. Harris edited the local paper. He carried on a friendly debate with Harris concerning the relative merits of the two lumber towns. John conceded Orange was predominant in schooner traffic, and he credited the town as "a live place" with "a good and energetic set of people." But Beaumont, he argued, was in another class. "We have produced over fifty million feet of lumber this year," he claimed, plus "a daily average of ten car loads of railroad ties." In addition, he bragged that "we ship an immense number of cattle and horses, and large amount of cleaned rice, brooms and leather."[16]

The prodigious lumber production claimed by John was confirmed during 1881 by a New Orleans newspaperman. Referring to Beaumont as "the timber center of Eastern Texas" and crediting the town with a "brilliant future," the writer ticked off the names of the local mills along with estimates of production. The five sawmills of Reliance, Beaumont Lumber, Smythe, Olive & Sternenberg, and Adams & Milmo together produced more than fifty million feet per year. The Williams planing mill dressed ten thousand feet annually. And the shingle mills of Long & Company and Olive & Sternenberg together turned out fifty million shingles on an annual basis. Total sales for all the Beaumont mills were estimated at $1,000,000 for the year 1881.[17]

The Beaumont and Orange lumber industry, impressive as it was, would have been even larger if more transportation had been available. During late 1880 and early 1881, the sawmill men of Southeast Texas complained about Texas & New Orleans Railroad's failure to furnish enough rail cars to handle the production at their local mills. John took up the cause of the lumbermen, sometimes irritating the T. & N.O. officials and also tweaking the Orange sawmill men who, John thought, were receiving preferential assignments of rail cars.[18]

For several months beginning in December 1880, John protested publicly to T. & N.O. about the shortage of rail cars. "We have the best lumber town in Texas," he argued, "but we might as well have no mills if we cannot market their product." He reported that the number of cars available for both Orange and Beaumont was only 280, a quantity he deemed "wholly insufficient." He recommended that if T. & N.O. did not furnish more cars, the sawmill men should develop a marine transportation system as an alternative, suggesting the use of barges and tugs to move the lumber to Sabine Pass and there connect with ocean shipping.[19]

John aggressively promoted the proposition of marine transportation for his town, campaigning for improvements in the Sabine-Neches waterway that would allow ocean shipping direct from Beaumont. He lobbied for deep water, claiming that the Neches all the way to Beaumont and the Sabine up to Orange already had twenty-five feet of water, plenty for ocean going vessels that could handle the lumber export trade. The only obstacle, he claimed, was the lack of deep water at the Sabine Pass bar and in Sabine Lake. He envisioned Beaumont as an ocean port and predicted, perhaps too optimistically, in his paper's January 1, 1881 issue that "we're going to be a better seaport than Galveston or Houston either."[20]

To promote the Sabine-Neches deep-water projects, he recommended that Beaumont business leaders join with their Orange counterparts to lobby Congress for appropriations for dredging at Sabine Pass. He wanted twenty-five feet at the pass and in the ship channel through the lake. Probably arousing the ire of Galveston and Houston interests, he claimed that a proposed $1 million appropriation for dredging at Galveston would be wasted and that the same money could be better spent at Sabine. He argued that digging in the "light sand" bottom at Galveston would produce only temporary improvements, while the same dredging in the mud bottom at Sabine Pass would be "permanent."[21]

John foresaw a grand future for the Sabine-Neches waterway, including the port at Sabine Pass. He boosted the development of the port in the January 22, 1881 issue, offering an open invitation to Jay Gould, the railroad developer, to choose Sabine Pass as the gulf outlet for his rail system. Explaining that it was "a safe, secure and practical harbor," he predicted that the Sabine Pass port would become "the best between Pensacola and Vera Cruz."[22]

Apparently John's campaign for more rail cars, along with his threat to convert to direct ocean shipping, helped produce positive results. By February 1881, he was reporting happily on T. & N.O. efforts to solve the car shortage, noting on February 5 that the company was constructing 150 new flat cars and, on February 12, that the car shortage was almost at an end, and finally that "the mills are preparing to chaw up their timber." He also applauded the railroad company for their announced plans to spend $750,000 to put the road in "first class condition."[23]

In addition to doing the job of an unofficial Beaumont chamber of commerce, John's paper served in the traditional role of town building, campaigning constantly for various civic and cultural improvements. He recommended the establishment of a fire fighting company, attended its organizational meeting, and was credited with giving the group its name, Beaumont Fire Company, No. 1. Observing that "Beaumont needs an opera house worthy of the name," he suggested the formation of a joint stock company, which he thought would be a good investment. He urged the organization of another joint stock company, this one for the development of Magnolia Cemetery, a three-acre public burial ground that had been donated to the town by rancher William McFaddin. John wanted to see the property enlarged and improved, so as to have a cemetery "worthy of the town."[24]

In other development campaigns, John, through his paper, promoted the improvement of drainage and roads in Beaumont. He urged county officials and local businessmen to dig better ditches and install more culverts, to drain rain water off into the river. He praised J. B. Langham, the county road commissioner, for development of new road-building techniques. An earlier method involved filling mud holes with sawdust and wood slabs taken from waste piles of the sawmills. The result, John recalled, was horrendous. "After rains, the horses stumbled on the slabs, malaria germs found breeding grounds in the rain-sodden sawdust, and the streets were in deplorable condition." Mr. Langham devised an improved system; he "plowed up Pearl street along its entire length, turned the earth with a scraper so as to crown the center and make as good a road as possible from the native mud and leave a drainage gutter on each side of the road."[25]

John's most important town-building task came during the spring and summer of 1881, when he promoted the official organization of a city government for Beaumont. The seventeenth Texas legislature had provided for the optional incorporation of towns with populations of between 1000 and 3000, which included Beaumont and Orange. John favored incorporation, declaring in the April 30 issue that he wanted his town to have "a good and efficient government." On June 25, he published the official resolution, which set forth proposed boundaries and petitioned the county judge to order an election for the incorporation of "The City of Beaumont."[26]

John urged voters to approve the proposition, explaining that incorporation was needed for improvements in roads, sanitation, public health, and law enforcement. Answering those who objected to the expense of government, he argued that the costs would be small when compared to the benefits. Several times he emphasized the need to improve law enforcement, citing problems presented by "drunken loafers," "wild boys," and others who roamed the streets, slept on sidewalks and railway platforms, and otherwise disturbed the lives of decent people. As an example, he reported a recent occurrence on Pearl Street, where "four persons, in the light of day, and without any concern for decency whatever, behaved in a way that is impossible to publish."[27]

Despite John's editorial urging, the voter turnout in the July 12 election was slight, and the margin of victory was very slim—a mere nine votes. Only 224 ballots were cast, with 115 in favor of the proposition, 107 against, and two left blank. "A close vote," John announced, "but we are a city." He was pleased with the election results but felt compelled to defend himself against an unnamed critic who had questioned his nationality and his right to participate in Beaumont's political affairs. "I am a citizen of the United States," he declared, adding that he had "lived in Beaumont seven years altogether" and expected to live there "seventy more." He further defied his critics, waving the flag of journalistic independence and declaring that "the paper will be neutral on nothing affecting the interests of our people."[28]

As soon as incorporation was approved, John began promoting the election of city officials, including a mayor and five aldermen. Initially, he adopted a non-partisan policy, vowing not to endorse specific candidates and asking only for the election of "good men" who had "good business qualifications." He published the names of three who filed for the mayor's position—Dr. J. W. Carlton, C. L. Sibley, and John C. Craig—and paid compliments to all three. Later John abandoned his neutrality, adding his personal endorsement to a "Citizens Ticket" composed of mayoral candidate John Craig and alderman prospects John Keith, Valery Blanchette, Lem P. Ogden, and Dr. J. A. Gilder. John judged this "a strong ticket" and signed his name to a list of eighty-five community leaders who publicly favored it.[29]

On August 13, the *Enterprise* announced the complete victory of the "Citizens Ticket," all members of the group winning election and being joined by F. E. Adams, who captured the fifth alderman position. John approved the results and predicted confidently that the new officials would conduct city affairs on "business principles." Again the vote was small, only 203. Somehow John had obtained the racial composition of the voters, because he reported that 180 whites and 123 African Americans had cast ballots. "The colored vote did not control the election," he declared simply, and with apparent satisfaction.[30]

John's remark about Beaumont's African American vote was typical of the racial attitudes displayed in his paper. In an article describing a racial incident, he revealed traditional prejudice toward blacks. James Land, a white man, had been attacked by two blacks, who knocked him off a sidewalk and cut at him with a knife. "The negroes are getting too impudent lately," John observed, "and we know of several cases in which they have insulted ladies and other respectable citizens."[31]

But at times his racial prejudice was softened by expressions of humanity and justice. In an August 6, 1881, article titled "A Sad Accident" he announced the death of Bob Jirou, an African American who had worked as a butcher and suffered a fatal accident while trying to rope a steer. "Bob was a very estimable colored man who was highly respected in the community both by white and black," John observed thoughtfully. "His remains were attended to the grave . . . by a large concourse of people." In another story appearing in the August 20 issue, John reported an incident in which a James Hill, a white man, had entered the house of a mulatto woman and "proceeded to indecently assault her." The woman had resisted his efforts, and the man retreated, "the enraged amazon" following in hot pursuit. "The chase was long, the effects bloody and severe, and finally ended in the capture and lodgement of the white scoundrel." John was indignant at the actions of the white man and recommended a long imprisonment as his punishment.[32]

Aside from covering Beaumont news, John devoted considerable attention to state and national affairs. During 1881, he furnished periodic reports about activities of the seventeenth state legislature, detailing various bills and sometimes taking editorial positions. He favored a proposed gun control measure, wanting "to abolish the pernicious and useless habit of carrying deadly weapons," a practice that he said had been the "cause of so much bloodshed in Texas." He lobbied against a proposed constitutional amendment that would prohibit the manufacture, distribution, and sale of intoxicating liquors; while conceding that "excess in liquor is a great evil," he estimated that the majority of voters would not approve such a proposition. On the much debated legislative questions about the location of the proposed state university and its medical department, he favored Austin for the site of the main institution and Houston for its medical branch.[33]

The most important national news in 1881 concerned the assassination of President James Garfield, whom John had described earlier as "a man of ability" and who, he thought, would be "as good a President as any Republican." Like most Americans, John was shocked at the shooting of Garfield by James Guiteau, a disgruntled office seeker. On July 9, he reported that the "dastardly act of Guiteau" had caused "a great excitement and indignation all over the state." During July and August he printed periodic bulletins about the President's condition; and on September 24 he advised his readers of Garfield's death, an event that caused "a feeling of sadness in the community." In the same edition he published a long article praising the slain president, announcing funeral arrangements, and quoting messages of condolence from Queen Victoria and the Lord Mayor of London.[34]

Sometimes John took pleasure in publicizing the activities of family members. On several occasions he mentioned that Cousin Will, "J. W. L. Johnson, Esq. of Orange," had visited the newspaper offices or attended court in Beaumont. On December 4, 1880, John proudly announced that he had hired Hannah's husband to work at the paper. "Mr. T. A. Lamb, late book-keeper for Reliance Lumber Company, has resigned his position and is connected with the *Enterprise* as its business manager."[35]

On November 27, 1880, John reported good news about Uncle Bob, stating that "the friends of R. H. Leonard will be glad to hear that he has resumed the practice of law." Apparently the elder Leonard had rebounded from his mental illness, at least enough to win approval from the local courts. Just one week earlier, Uncle Bob had represented himself in an ex parte case in which he asked the county court to set aside the 1877 order that had found him insane and committed him to the Austin asylum. After hearing testimony in this latest case, the jury determined that Leonard was "of sound mind and fully capable of attending to his affairs."[36]

Soon after overcoming his insanity, allegedly "caused" by religion and spiritualism, Robert Leonard plunged again into religious matters. This time Uncle Bob involved himself in the Darwinian controversies that plagued Christian society in Great Britain and America. Charles Darwin's theories about evolution and natural selection, published in the *Origin of the Species* (1859) and in the *Descent of Man* (1871), were seen by many Christians as a direct challenge to Biblical truths about man and his world. Reactions to Darwinian theories among Christians were various, ranging from outright rejection to measured acceptance, attempting to reconcile the theories with traditional religious doctrine. Among the Americans arguing in favor of reconciliation were Massachusetts Congregationalist minister Henry Ward Beecher and Harvard naturalist Asa Gray, both of whom suggested that evolution was God's process and natural selection was a divine power.[37]

Uncle Bob, a devoted Methodist, took up the challenge in Beaumont, making several "Creation" speeches in which he attempted to reconcile the latest scientific developments with traditional Christianity. On December 18, 1880, the *Enterprise* announced his first offering, a lecture delivered at a fund raising event for the Mission of the Good Shepherd, the Episcopal church that John was helping establish. "Amacus," an anonymous writer for the paper, offered a glowing account of Leonard's one and one-half hour address:

> He planted himself squarely on the Bible and from this high stand
> point surveyed the entire field of scientific discovery, examining in turn
> the different schools of thought and the various theories advanced,
> showing them to be untenable because in conflict with Divine Truth, and

by the scientific method harmonized Religion and Science, and reconciled, by a Theory peculiarly his own, all scientific discovery yet made
with the Mosaic account of The Creation. . . . In this masterly effort, the
lecturer showed himself to be, not only a professional scholar and deep
thinker, but also a well raised close student—thoroughly conversant with
the current literature of the time. . . . The lecture was a gentle and grace-
ful flow of chaste and elegant language, without a hitch or a jar to mar the
beauty of the argument or the electrical effect on the audience.

After closing his lecture, Robert Leonard returned to his seat "amid applause and hearty congratulations" and enjoying a "unanimous verdict—
Well done."[38]

John Leonard derived various benefits from the operation of his newspaper, both financial and personal. Business records for the *Enterprise* are
not available, but it appears likely that it was profitable, at least after the initial start-up period. During the first year, the paper enjoyed a healthy increase in advertising revenues, with its number of paid columns increasing
from three to eleven. Later John claimed the paper was a successful venture,
stating that when he subsequently relinquished control to Tom Lamb, the
operation was free of encumbrances except for "a debt of a few hundred
dollars due to a printer's supply house in Houston."[39]

Being a professional journalist qualified John for membership in the
Bohemian Society, a statewide fraternity of newspapermen. This group had
many potential members; in 1880 Texas counted 280 newspapers, including 30 dailies and 231 weeklies, such as the *Enterprise.* On February 5, 1881,
John reported having visited Houston and had "the honor of being introduced to the Bohemian Society." There he met a number of the city's leading newspapermen, including Gail B. Johnson, "Professor" T. J. Giradeau,
D. D. Bryan and Hamp Cook, all associated with the *Houston Post.* Later,
on April 30, he described another trip to Houston, when he performed the
duty required of all Bohemians, paying calls on various fellow journalists,
this time meeting Dan H. "Uncle Dan" McGary, owner and editor of the
Houston Age. From Houston he embarked on a "ramble," visiting East and
Central Texas towns, such as Palestine, Austin, and San Antonio, and
meeting various newsmen. In the Alamo City he enjoyed making the acquaintance of James P. Newcomb, the former Radical Republican newspaperman who was then publishing the *Evening Light.* On May 21, John
expressed thanks for Newcomb's hospitality, acknowledging "great obliga-
tions for courtesies extended."[40]

Being proprietor of the *Enterprise* also permitted John to become a member of the Texas Press Association. In May 1881, he traveled to Houston to attend the second annual meeting of that group. He heard an "excellent" speech by Col. George H. Sweet of the *Galveston Journal,* participated in election of officers, and voted in favor of a proposition that would limit membership to "publishers and actual editors." The association had already selected Houston for its next meeting, and John, himself an accomplished booster, complimented the city for promoting itself and for its "enterprise and far-sighted business tact."[41]

John enjoyed the comradeship of fellow newspapermen, exchanging newspapers, borrowing articles, and trading compliments. Soon after getting out his first few issues, he received encouraging words from various papers. The *Houston Post* thought the *Enterprise* was "judiciously edited," the *Morgan City Review* (Louisiana) suggested that the paper "deserves to be well patronized," and the *Orange Tribune* observed that it presented a "first class appearance." John often returned the compliments, on one occasion doffing his hat to *Orange Tribune* editor A. P. Harris and describing his paper as "live, wide awake and progressive."[42]

Carrying on a friendly competition with this same editor, John referred to him as "Brother Harris," read his paper, and sometimes offered free advice about crime and violence that plagued the town of Orange. Early in 1881, while discussing problems of lawlessness, he praised the Orange Rifles, a volunteer militia "composed of the best citizens," including his friend Harris and his cousin Will. Such a group was sorely needed, he declared, because Orange could no longer afford "the unenviable reputation of being the home of the worst set of roughs and rowdies in East Texas."[43]

During August 1881, John returned to the subject of crime in Orange, this time covering "The Orange Trouble," a riot that drew considerable coverage in Galveston and Houston papers. The trouble apparently arose from an ongoing dispute between Sheriff George Michael and Charles Delano, a butcher who reportedly directed the criminal activities of a group of African Americans, including the Saxon brothers, Robert and Sam. The dispute erupted into violence when the Saxons ambushed the sheriff, wounding him with gunfire. A riot ensued in which outraged Orange citizens captured Delano and killed the Saxon brothers, hanging Robert and shooting Sam. The Orange Rifles were mobilized and order was restored, but the incident further soiled the already ugly reputation of the town.[44]

The *Houston Daily Post* weighed in, condemning Orange for "its evil reputation" that derived from the "many murders and . . . the general cussedness of a minority of the people." There, "the laws of the land" were "mocked by a gang of irresponsible rowdies." Hinting at the possible need for "a vigilance committee," the Houston paper urged "the citizens to clear their skirts of the murder of innocent men and women . . . and take steps to remove the unenviable reputation . . . which works against their development as a law-respecting and moral people."[45]

John followed the same line, condemning "The Outrages at Orange" and urging respectable citizens to get rid of the trouble-making rowdies. But he added new allegations, charging that monied and so-called prominent people were in league with the lawbreakers and suggesting that the justice system was corrupt: "The rowdy element contains some men of means, and criminals have little difficulty in giving bonds, and when offenses culminate in the semblance of a trial, . . . an acquittal is almost certain." He urged the good citizens of Orange to "crush this diabolical set of wretches, who are the curse and disgrace of the town." Soon, the problem of lawlessness in Orange would touch John himself.[46]

CHAPTER 10

GONE FROM TEXAS

On October 29, 1881, John Leonard celebrated his paper's first birthday with a lead editorial, "To Our Readers." Remarking on the "rapid strides" achieved by the *Enterprise,* he expressed "deep gratitude" to the "solid businessmen of Beaumont" for "generous and appreciative support." He pointed with pride "to the city's rapid growth," promising to strive to make the paper "a true champion of her interests" and proposing "to carry out the programme . . . to build up South-East Texas with all our power." Relations with patrons had been "most pleasant," he noted. "We hope to continue for many years to come."[1]

In the same issue, John offered a breezy account of a just-completed trip to Orange. He had called on his friend "Brother Harris"—*Tribune* editor and "genial gentleman." He also had visited Brazeale's Lone Star Saloon, "a favorite resort"; Wingate's lumber mill, noting "all the modern improvements in machinery"; and Greeve's foundry, "fast becoming one of the leading institutions of South East Texas."[2]

"On Wednesday morning," he continued, "professional business called us to the court house." But he did not tell the whole story about the "professional business." The truth was that Will Johnson was in trouble, and John had gone to help him. Cousin Will had been indicted by an Orange County grand jury on a charge of "Theft of filed papers." Listed as No. 616, the case was styled *State of Texas v. J. W. L. Johnson.* Details of the charge, including the nature of the "filed papers," have not been learned but it probably arose out of Will's law practice. Perhaps he was accused of stealing court papers in order to help a client, or removing a surety bond that had been given by a friend or associate. In any event, the charge was not a trivial matter; conviction carried a minimum prison sentence of three years.[3]

On October 26, John appeared with Will in the Orange County District Court, John being listed as "surety and family" and Will as principal. Together, they posted a $500 bail bond, an instrument that kept Will out of jail, pending resolution of the case. The bond guaranteed that Will would "appear before the District Court of Orange County now in session . . . and there remain from day to day and time to time and not depart without leave of the Court."[4]

What happened to Will Johnson and John Leonard after they stood together that day in the Orange court is a mystery. They both left the Beaumont area within about twenty-four months, but exact details of why and when are not clear. Historical records pertaining to these questions are scarce. File papers for Case No. 616 have disappeared, and other court records provide only the barest information. Mysteriously, after October 29, 1881, all issues of the *Enterprise* are missing for a period of seventeen years, even though the paper was published continually during that period. There are no family letters, except two written by Will Johnson in October 1882. John, who later wrote so much about his Beaumont years, never referred to Case No. 616 and hardly ever mentioned Will's name. Little remains but the skeletal court records and vestiges of old family stories.[5]

On October 31, five days after Will and John posted the bail bond, there were more developments in Case No. 616. Gambler and saloon keeper H. McDowell, who earlier had been acquitted of murder, was called into court as "a witness for the defendant." In Will's case, McDowell posted a $500 bond guaranteeing "to personally appear before the District Court . . . on the 3d Monday in April . . . to testify on behalf of the defendant." The connection between Will and McDowell has not been learned, but possibly it had to do with McDowell's trial and acquittal. He had been acquitted on April 20, 1880, and Will was indicted on May 3, only thirteen days later. The proximity in time of the two developments makes a presumption of connection almost irresistible. Had Will filched court papers and thereby somehow allowed McDowell to go free?[6]

Court action on Will's case was delayed repeatedly. At the April 1882 term of the court, the case was "continued as on affidavit of defendant," meaning action was deferred until the next court session. Why it was postponed is not known. Perhaps McDowell did not appear. Maybe Will requested a delay, pleading he was not ready for trial. The records do not show whether Will acted as his own attorney or was represented by another lawyer, such as one of his Orange associates or perhaps John or Uncle Bob. Uncle Bob would be a reasonable guess, given his long experience in criminal matters and his loyalty to his nephew, which apparently remained intact up to the end.[7]

John left Beaumont in 1882 because of health problems, or at least that was his explanation when writing many years after the events. "My health broke down. I was again a victim of malaria and was advised to change climates. I hated leaving Beaumont but had to go, leaving behind my sister and many relatives and friends." But probably sickness was not the only reason that caused him to leave. In 1873 he had left Beaumont "because of his health," but that departure had coincided with personal problems, the controversies surrounding the Luder case and the failure of his marriage to Annie. Now, perhaps he was embarrassed or somehow threatened by Will's trouble. For whatever reasons, John did leave the town and would not set foot again in the place until 1927, forty-five years later.[8]

At the next regular term of the court in October 1882, Will's case was brought up again, and again it was "continued as on affidavit of defendant." Apparently, the local district attorney and whoever represented Will agreed to a delay. Were they looking for McDowell?[9]

On October 16, 1882, Will wrote to Viola in Woodville, McCraken County, Kentucky. Sometime earlier she had taken the children and gone there for a long visit, reportedly to see relatives and to consult a trusted physician about a chronic health problem of her own. She probably suffered from consumption, the cause of her death many years later. Will's letter was brief, its tone subdued but loving. "My Own Darling," he wrote, "Well, here I am once again. I find Orange very dull." He added, "Court commenced this morning. Everything looks all right," perhaps alluding to Case No. 616.[10]

The letter also reported to Viola about a house they owned in Beaumont and rented to a "Mr. Morris," who apparently had not been a satisfactory tenant: "I am going over to Beaumont tonight. I understand that Mr. Morris has left our place. . . . Uncle Bob is here, and goes back to Beaumont with me tonight. He says that he thinks I can sell the place without much trouble. Did you get any money from Morris? He told Uncle Bob that he had sent it." Obviously, Will was still close to Uncle Bob, depending on him for advice and probably legal counsel. Will closed his letter with words of love and affection. "Kiss the babies for papa, and take good care of yourself and keep cheerful. . . . Well, goodbye darling—will write again in a day or two from Beaumont."

Two weeks later Will wrote to Viola from Beaumont, on this occasion composing a longer letter from which pages are missing. This is the last extant correspondence from Will to Viola. Sometime after sending this letter, Will took a horrendous step—he ran away, abandoning Viola and his children, and severing relations for all time with Uncle Bob, friends, and family. His reasons for taking this tragic action are not clear. Certainly, he was pessimistic about his business prospects—and probably gloomy about his case's chances, perhaps thinking he might be convicted and sent to prison.

But were there other reasons? Additional charges of professional malfeasance? Financial woes? Mental illness? Adultery? Trouble with Viola's brothers? Family stories say that Lem and Ed drove him away, threatening to kill him if he did not leave. If so, what would have caused them to take such drastic action? Were they somehow mixed up with Will's case? or did his trial cause them embarrassment? There is no documentary evidence to support any of these other possibilities.

Will's last letter to Viola was written from Beaumont and dated October 29, 1882. Addressing her affectionately as "My Own Darling," he acknowledged her recent letter and its good news about her improving health: "I have just received your letter of October 24th, the first one I have yet received. I am extremely glad to know that you are better, and I hope you will continue to improve until at last day you may truly say 'I am well.'" He returned to the subject of Mr. Morris, reporting with considerable frustration that he had spoken to the man about past-due rent and damages to their house and property. He and Morris had argued about fixtures that had been ruined and others that had disappeared, until Will turned "thoroughly disgusted."[11]

He sent news about Viola's brothers, telling her of their efforts to obtain a government job connected with the construction of a jetty at Sabine Pass. "I believe I told you Lem and Ed were interested with Mr. Junker in the brush contract for Sabine Pass. It is supposed that they are really the main parties, and I reckon that supposition is about correct." The "brush contract" involved furnishing brush to be used as filler in the foundation of the new jetty. Wilson Junker, the Orange saloon keeper who had put up a surety bond for Will when he received the tax assessor's job, was Lem Ogden's brother-in-law and an apparent business partner. From Will's comments, it seems that the men's efforts to get the job might have involved an element of subterfuge.[12]

Turning to personal matters and becoming very serious, he wrote of their future life, referring to earlier discussions about the possibility of moving back to Beaumont or relocating to a new town altogether. "I have about given out the idea of returning to Beaumont, as I know you do not want to live here, and I am not in love with the place." If Will and Viola were thinking about leaving the Beaumont area, perhaps her brothers opposed the idea and would not let her go.

Will closed his last letter with professions of love for Viola and their children, Mittie, Ogden, and Alma, then ages eight, six, and three. Also, while revealing that he had already visited them in Kentucky, he promised to come again in the near future. In these final words he betrayed no hint of weakness in his commitment to Viola and his family. He still loved his children, still felt passion for his wife: "I am glad to know all the babies are well, especially that Ogden is getting fat. Tell Miss Alma I will be back to Kentucky soon. I am not going to stay here much longer. . . . Give my love to all. Kiss the babies for papa as usual, and when I come I will kiss you for myself. Ever Your Own. Willie."

But Will did not keep his word. According to the family story, when Viola and the children made their return trip to Beaumont, they traveled by way of New Orleans where Will had promised to meet them. When they arrived in the Crescent City, Viola was met instead by her brothers, Lem and Ed. Will Johnson was gone from Texas—gone forever.[13]

FOLLOWING
DIFFERENT PATHS

After leaving Texas, both Will Johnson and John Leonard lived by their pens, but they followed very different paths. Will was running away, abandoning wife and children; he started a new life, changed his name, and embarked on a journalistic odyssey, working his way across the world as a newspaperman. John also started a new life, but he pursued more conventional means. After brief newspaper stints in New Orleans and Memphis, he moved to Chicago in 1883 and went to work for the *Chicago Daily Telegram.* In 1884 he married Georgiana Meeker of Rochelle, Illinois, and started a family, ultimately having five children: Howard, Bessie, Alice, Robert, and William.[1]

John served three years as an editor of the *Daily Telegram,* after which he launched out on a free-lance writing career. He was an adept and prolific writer for hire, producing more than fifty books and countless articles and columns. He wrote histories of various cities, newspapers, and business corporations, often traveling about the country to gather material. Among his titles were *Industries of Detroit, Centennial Review of Cincinnati,* and *Gold Fields of the Klondike.*[2]

He developed special skills as a compiler of directories and created the first *Who's Who* volume in the United States. Many years earlier he had seen such directories in England and in 1887 proposed an American edition to A. N. Marquis, the Chicago publisher. Marquis accepted the proposition, and in 1899 they published the first *Who's Who in America.* The volume was well received, and John served as editor of four subsequent biennial editions. For Marquis he also directed publication of various city biographical directories, such as *The Book of Chicagoans* and *The Book of St. Louisans.*[3]

John involved himself in Illinois politics, working within the ranks of the Democratic Party and even seeking office for himself. He attended the Democratic State Conventions of 1898 and 1900, both years winning the nomination for the U.S. Congress for the Eighth Illinois District. "It was a Republican district," Mrs. Leonard explained later, "so he didn't win."

John agreed with his wife's analysis, consoling himself with the observation that "I polled more votes than any Democrat had before."[4]

A dispute with Marquis about admission of biographies in *Who's Who* caused John to break relations with the Chicago publisher. In 1906 he moved his family to New York City, where he joined L. R. Hammersly Company, publisher of *Who's Who in New York*. In association with Hammersly and other publishers, John produced a series of specialized *Who's Who* volumes, featuring notables in finance, jurisprudence, and engineering, and including *Women's Who's Who of America*. He also wrote a variety of historical books covering America's maritime operations, the petroleum industry, the U.S. Marines, the Episcopal Church, and the city of New York.[5]

For the *Beaumont Enterprise,* the paper he had founded, John produced "Uncle Willie's Column," a weekly commentary that covered contemporary American politics and the history of Southeast Texas. During 1928–32, he wrote more than two hundred of these columns, many of them recalling his adventures in Beaumont. "Uncle Willie" regaled his readers with many interesting and humorous stories about his experiences as a school teacher, lawyer, and newspaperman. But John omitted from his column any mention of embarrassing episodes, such as his marriage to Annie, the Jacob Luder case, or his close involvement with Will's troubles.[6]

John lived to a ripe old age of eighty-three, remaining a loyal Democrat to the time of his death. He eagerly followed the party's activities, pledging to "always stay a Democrat," but complaining that "most of the good Democrats are dead." He resented many of the party newcomers, such as Franklin D. Roosevelt, saying "there's a lot of them nowadays I can't vote for." Listening on the radio to the 1932 Democratic Convention, he monitored his party's actions, including the nomination of Roosevelt as president. On the afternoon of June 30, soon after one of the convention broadcasts, he suffered a heart attack and died.[7]

His funeral services were conducted under the auspices of New York City's Grace Methodist Episcopal Church. In 1896, John had given up the Anglican Church and become an ardent Methodist, serving several years as a church trustee and for a long time holding a preacher's license. His passing received generous coverage in the *Beaumont Enterprise* and in four New York papers, including the *Herald Tribune,* which noted his many and diverse accomplishments as "editor, publisher, sailor, historian, prospector, author, and lawyer."[8]

While living in Chicago and New York, John had witnessed from afar the deaths of all the other members of the Leonard-John-Lamb clan. Uncle

Bob, the original head of the immigrant families, had been the first to pass away, dying in 1892 at the age of fifty-eight. After John and Will left Beaumont, Bob Leonard continued practicing law and apparently suffered no more episodes of insanity. He also engaged in the real estate business, buying and selling numerous parcels of land and developing several small subdivisions in the town. His second wife, Rosalie, died in 1887, and he married again two years later to Fannie Morris. He and Fannie had a daughter, Ester, bringing the number of his natural children to nine, six of whom survived him. Obituaries in Houston papers noted Robert Leonard's passing, describing him as "a prominent lawyer and one of Beaumont's oldest citizens" and reporting that his funeral was "largely attended by bar and citizens."[9]

Tom Lamb died in 1917 at age seventy-five, having spent the last thirty years of his life in the printing business. Sometime after John left Beaumont, Tom gave up his interest in the *Beaumont Enterprise* and became a professional printer. He helped organize the Beaumont Typographical Union and in 1895 founded the Lamb Printing Company, later passing ownership of that company to one of his sons. He and his wife, Hannah, remained devoted members of Saint Mark's Episcopal Church. They always sang in the choir, and he served many years on the vestry. At the time of his death, the Beaumont paper praised Tom Lamb as "one of Beaumont's most beloved citizens," a "quiet and unassuming" man who "made friends readily and held them."[10]

Hannah passed away six years later, on September 12, 1923, at the age of eighty. Described in a Beaumont newspaper as a "pioneer of the city," she was remembered as a teacher and musician, who had greatly influenced the cultural and religious life of the town. In 1895 she had helped organize the Beaumont Literary Club, a group that subsequently became the Women's Reading Club and finally the Women's Club of Beaumont. Hannah was survived by five children, numerous grandchildren, and her brother, John Leonard.[11]

John did not attend Hannah's funeral, but he traveled to Beaumont four years later, called back to the area to testify in a Hardin County land dispute. He arrived in January 1927, seeing the town for the first time in forty-five years, a curiously long absence given his oft-expressed affection for his sister and her children. Staying almost a month, he did plenty of catching up with friends and family, and probably met with officials of the *Beaumont Enterprise* to discuss the "Uncle Willie's" column that he would write for the paper. By a curious coincidence, he was in town when Viola Johnson died on January 19 and must have attended her funeral.[12]

He became friendly with Viola's children Ogden and Alma, now young adults, and from Ogden he probably heard about Viola's life and her financial struggles. John also must have learned that Ogden harbored hostile feelings against his father, blaming him for his mother's misfortunes. After Will's disappearance, Viola had fallen on hard times. Likely estranged for a time from her brothers, Lem and Ed—perhaps because of their cruel treatment of her husband—she did not receive financial support from them; nor did she return to Lem's household, where she had lived before her marriage.[13]

She and her children resided in a small house in a poor neighborhood. Viola performed menial tasks to raise money, taking in sewing, sitting with sick people, and laying out the dead. She posted death notices around town, attaching the black-bordered announcements to poles and fences. For years, she had no money for extras. Alma, her younger daughter, remembered those difficult days, at one time desperately wanting a pair of stylish shoes and being crushed by her mother's refusal to buy them.[14]

Viola began divorce proceedings against Will in September 1886, about three years after he disappeared. In papers filed by her attorneys, she charged that he had abandoned her and their children about August 1, 1882, and never returned. Her petition further claimed that she "performed her duties . . . in a wifely manner" but that he "totally disregarded his marital vows." This charge against him might have been a real complaint or standard language used to perfect the divorce case. She made none of the other complaints often seen in divorce papers, such as cruelty, alcoholism, or adultery. Tom Lamb and Lem Ogden appeared as witnesses for Viola, both merely confirming basic facts of the couple's marriage and separation. Will's court-appointed lawyers denied the allegations, but on May 21, 1887, the court granted Viola the divorce and awarded her custody of the three children.[15]

Lem's appearance as a witness on his sister's behalf probably signaled an end to the estrangement between Viola and her brothers. What prompted the reconciliation is not known for sure. Perhaps her anger against them subsided; possibly they gave her cash to make amends for having driven Will away, or maybe they helped her find ways to make money in the land business. By 1895, she was engaged in her own name in real estate development, an activity derived directly from property she and her brothers inherited from their father and mother. That year she was involved in land transactions with her brothers; she also began selling town lots in the Johnson Addition, a tract taken from the original Ogden homestead.[16]

In March 1895, Viola's daughter Mittie married L. I. Parminter, a Reliance Lumber Company clerk born in New Jersey. Conducted by local

Episcopal rector H. P. Vicborn, the wedding service was held in the parlor at Lem's house—further evidence that Viola and her brother were reconciled. Unfortunately, Mittie passed away while still a young woman, dying in childbirth in 1900 at age twenty-five.[17]

In July 1901, Viola filed an official plat with the county clerk for her Johnson Addition, a subdivision then comprising thirty new town lots along Pennsylvania and Sabine Pass Avenues. Her property turned into a prime development, situated close to downtown Beaumont and officially coming on the market only six months after the January 10 discovery of the fabulous Spindletop oil gusher. Development of the Spindletop oil field ignited an economic boom in Beaumont; the population surged, land values soared, and prosperity favored many local citizens, including Viola.[18]

She built a fine residence for herself in the Johnson Addition, taking two lots that fronted on Sabine Pass Avenue. The East Texas plantation-style house was large, more than six thousand square feet and two and one-half stories, with a wide front porch, tall columns, and twin chimneys. The entry featured a divided stairway, and the second floor had five bedrooms, each with its own fireplace. The third floor contained a spacious ballroom.[19] Viola's new house was grand, if not grandiose, and certainly beyond the practical needs of a widow and two grown children. Her construction of such a place may have been a statement to the town and perhaps to her brothers, a public declaration of pride and revenge.

She and her children thoroughly enjoyed their new residence. Ogden and Alma hosted parties there and became much involved with the town's young social set, helping organize "secret clubs" such as the "Jolly Boys of Beaumont" and "Just Us Girls." In 1901, Ogden married Lomie Salter, a newcomer from Florida, and moved her into the family house. While residing there, Lomie gave birth on April 5, 1904, to the couple's only child, Viola's only natural grandchild, a girl named Mittie. It was while living in relative luxury on Sabine Pass Avenue that Viola heard the shocking news of Will's death—that he had died a disabled pauper.[20]

Viola sold the Sabine Pass property in 1906 for $10,250, a handsome sum in those days, and moved the family to a new cottage on Park Street. There, in 1907, Alma married I. W. Lawhon, a Beaumont lawyer, in services conducted by J. W. White, pastor of First Baptist Church. The new Lawhon couple set up housekeeping elsewhere, but Viola continued living on Park Street with Ogden and his family. Beginning in those times and for the rest of her days, she identified herself as the "widow" of J. W. L. Johnson. Perhaps she maintained this identification for social convenience, widowed being more acceptable than abandoned and divorced, or maybe she still cared for Will.[21]

By 1921 Viola was residing on Liberty Street with Alma and her husband and their two-year-old adopted daughter, Doris. When Viola had moved to the Lawhon residence, she paid for construction of her own room, specially designed with seven large windows. She suffered from consumption and had been advised by doctors to get plenty of fresh air. During 1926 she weakened, spending much of her time in bed. For hours on end, she lay quietly next to four windows, watching birds that she fed on a window ledge.[22]

Viola died on January 19, 1927, at age eighty, having outlived Will by more than twenty years. She was buried in Magnolia Cemetery next to her daughter, Mittie. Her estate, valued at more than $39,000, was left equally to Ogden and Alma. Among her personal belongings were numerous mementos from her life with Will: photographs of his family in King's Lynn and portraits of Will and herself. There were seven letters from his sister, Sarah Ann, two from John and one from Uncle Bob. And there were Will's letters addressed to her—the love letter from 1873 and the two from 1882, written just before he disappeared. She must have read his letters again and again, reliving those days and trying to reconcile herself to the heartbreaking disappointments of her life. She also must have pondered long about Will's strange and tragic life after he left Beaumont.[23]

She had learned something about him from California newspaper obituaries. After departing from Texas, Will had gone to Panama in Central America. Exactly when he went there, or when he changed his name, is not known. Somehow he had obtained a connection with the *New York Star,* which sent him to cover the efforts of Ferdinand de Lesseps to construct the Panama Canal. In Panama City, Will assumed the name James W. Leonard and was hired by the *Panama Star and Herald,* a daily paper that covered the canal project with editions in English, Spanish, and French.

De Lesseps, the celebrated builder of the Suez Canal, and his Panama project attracted worldwide attention. During 1881–89, he and his French organization, the Universal Interoceanic Canal Company, attempted to excavate a fifty mile sea-level canal across the isthmus, from Panama City on the Pacific Ocean to Colon on the Atlantic. His bold and ambitious plan ended in failure, however, defeated by a variety of factors, including disease, inadequate equipment, and the impracticality of the sea-level plan.[24]

During its peak, the de Lesseps project brought thousands of people, including Will Johnson and other adventurers, to Panama City and the area. In 1884, the number of construction workers rose to approximately 20,000, about eighty percent being Indians and blacks from the Caribbean Islands. With the surge in population came attendant human problems; malaria, yellow fever, and other diseases ran rampant, claiming thousands of lives. Social conditions became chaotic: murders, barroom brawls, and riots were common, as was drunkenness and other forms of vice. Aside from the actual canal work, the most thriving industries were gambling houses, brothels, and coffin manufacturing.[25]

Now posing as "Mr. Leonard," Will became the editor of the English version of the *Star and Herald*. Putting out the paper on a daily basis required him to work long hours, but it also sharpened his journalistic skills. He worked hard and played hard, perhaps enjoying himself in the company of "ladies of leisure" and, as he readily admitted, "learning to drink champagne in lieu of water."[26]

After Panama, Will traveled across the Pacific, spending time first in Australia and later Hawaii, finding employment in both places as a journalist. In about 1887, he landed in San Francisco, where he worked several years for the *San Francisco Examiner*. He also served as a correspondent for magazines, writing articles for *Scribner's* and *Harper's Weekly*. Later, he moved down the coast, first to Santa Barbara, then to Ventura, in both towns writing as a correspondent for the *Examiner*.[27]

In August 1890, Will became a publisher, joining with California newspaperman Ben A. Sykes to operate the popular *Ventura Free Press*. Having already worked several months for the paper, Will was described as "well versed in newspaper work." In their salutary column, Leonard and Sykes promised to produce "a thorough Republican paper, devoted at all times to the best interests of the party." Will probably smiled secretly at his new Republican affiliations, remembering his harsh condemnation of the party as a Democrat in Texas. He and Sykes also vowed to "give all the news" and "at the same time have a proper regard for the moral tone of the community." He must have winced at his own hypocrisy, posing as a guardian of local morality while guilty himself of gross immoral deception.[28]

Will lasted only four months as publisher, stepping down on January 13, 1891. He yielded his place in the partnership to Alf D. Bowen, a young Republican who was introduced in the paper as "a sober, industrious and intelligent gentleman." Perhaps mention of Bowen's sobriety was perfunctory, or maybe it was purposeful, to contrast with Will whose work habits might have suffered from excessive drinking.[29]

Will quickly resumed his career as a journalist, a profession in which he was often recognized as "brilliant." He also changed his personal life, persuading a respectable young woman to become his wife. Bernice Pelham, a twenty-one-year-old school teacher living in Bakersfield, was described as "pretty" and credited with "a thoughtful and kindly disposition." She was one of two daughters of Oren and Mary Pelham of Santa Barbara. Their other daughter, Pauline, was married to Samuel T. Black, an English native who became prominent as an educator in southern California. The Pelhams did not approve the match, but Will persevered, employing all his charms and cleverness and winning Bernice "against the most aggressive opposition of her own family."[30]

Will and Bernice were married in her family's home in Santa Barbara on January 3, 1892. A friendly newsman in nearby Bakersfield congratulated the newlyweds, commenting that "if Mr. Leonard makes as good a husband as he has shown himself to be a writer, Mrs. Leonard will have no cause to regret her choice." Of course, there were causes of regret lurking in the background; the young woman did not know that her talented "Mr. Leonard" was actually Mr. Johnson, who was suppressing important facts about his earlier life. What was Will's state of mind when he and Bernice stood before the minister? Did he think he was committing bigamy, or did he know that Viola had divorced him?[31]

The young couple settled in Bakersfield where they continued their respective careers. In an 1892–93 statewide census, Will listed himself as "James William Leonard," journalist, "age 38," with "Nativity" in Texas. Obviously he had concocted a life story that reduced his age by two years and denied his English birth. He was hired as an associate editor by the *Bakersfield Democrat,* the new employment receiving warm comment in another local paper. Noting Will's previous newspaper experience in Panama, the fellow newsman declared, "he is heartily welcomed to the fraternity." He worked hard for the *Democrat* and was recognized as "a thorough newsman," who wielded "a trenchant and sometimes truculent pen" on behalf of the paper's editorial causes.[32]

Will idolized Bernice, becoming a good husband and a better man because of her. Given his new diligence on the job and at home, he likely controlled his drinking and took better care of his health. Residing in a Bakersfield hotel, they enjoyed their married life and socialized in the town. According to a local paper, they became leading members of the Pierian Club, a "really remarkable" literary organization in which he was recognized as "one of the bright intellects."[33]

But Will soon lost Bernice. The *Ventura Free Press* would later report that she "contracted a severe cold, which settled upon her lungs." Hoping to save her by a change in climate, he moved her from Bakersfield to her parents' home in Ventura. "But the seeds of that dread disease, consumption, had been sown." Will and the family lavished loving care upon her, but all they could do was try to make her comfortable. She died on April 13, 1895; her funeral services at Saint Paul's Episcopal Church in Ventura were attended by "a large number of sorrowing friends."[34]

Bernice's death was a crushing blow to Will. Sickened by sadness and loneliness, he resumed his heavy drinking, lost his job, and soon ran out of money. Four months after her funeral, he dragged himself to the Ventura cemetery and collapsed upon her grave, suffering from some kind of paralysis. Then only forty-three years old, he was carried to the county hospital and there committed, "a paralytic condemned to a living death."[35]

The Ventura County Hospital was a neat two-story white building that looked west from a prominent hillside. From there, the patients could enjoy pleasant views of the town rooftops and the blue waters of the Pacific Ocean. Less pleasant, certainly for Will, was the sight just across the street—the tree-studded cemetery bristling with tombstones. In 1900, the hospital had five staff persons and twenty-three "inmates," including Will, who now correctly stated his age as forty-seven but still claimed Texas as his birthplace.[36]

Apparently he was not physically paralysed, but emotionally broken and disabled by a variety of maladies: alcoholism, depression, and maybe insanity. He must have suffered terribly from guilt and sadness, having first deserted Viola and his children, then deceived and lost his precious Bernice. A strangely passive patient, he remained virtually silent and declined steadfastly to discuss his life or problems. He demanded to be known as "J. W. Leonard," refusing to permit use of his given names and at all times hiding his true identity from the hospital staff.[37]

According to the *Bakersfield Daily Californian*, Will survived nine long years, "a useless, forsaken derelict," rarely breaking his silence. On one occasion, he confided part of his story to a fellow patient, but only after swearing him to secrecy. As his death drew near, Will suffered "an uneasiness, a restlessness" which could only be soothed by divulging "the secret which had tormented him in the closing years of his life." Whether spurred by "contrition alone, or the ghastly vision of Potter's field, or both," he confessed. "Already long past the eleventh hour," he confided his story to hospital personnel, and they in turn rushed a telegraph message to his family in Beaumont.[38]

But it was to no avail; Viola and her son Ogden did not care or perhaps did not understand, possibly thinking that Will wanted to come home to

Viola. Or maybe they disagreed over what to do. According to family leg-
end, Ogden, who had grown to hate his father, handled the matter. He sent
Will a chilling message: "You can go anywhere in the world, but if you
come to Beaumont, I *will* kill you." Whether Will ever received this reply is
not known. He died March 3, 1904, and was buried without ceremony or
mourners, his remains consigned to "an unadorned pine box," carried
across the street, and laid away in a pauper's grave.[39]

Soon, newspapermen in Ventura, Bakersfield, and Santa Barbara picked
up the juicy story. The man they had known years ago as James W. Leonard,
who had married Bernice Pelham, was really J. W. L. Johnson, who had a
wife and children in Texas. They quickly assumed Will had committed
bigamy, that he had greatly wronged Bernice, "an innocent woman" whose
early death had spared her "the anguish of a domestic scandal."[40]

Within a few days, a letter to the editor of the *Ventura Free Press* set the
record straight. It was sent from Beaumont by Joanna Curtis, a close friend
of Viola Johnson. Writing "at the earnest solicitation of [Will's] first wife,"
Joanna explained that Will had in fact been divorced from Viola before marrying his second wife. Viola insisted that Bernice's innocent name be saved
and remain forever "stainless."[41]

Several papers printed Joanna's letter, including the *Bakersfield Daily
Californian,* which also published a long article, "The Life Tragedy of
J. W. Leonard." The writer, obviously a former comrade, sketched out
Will's "strange romantic story," remembering him with compassion, alluding to his faults but giving him full credit for his personal and professional
qualities. The late James Leonard, now identified as Will Johnson, was a
man of "great personal magnetism," "so popular that his society was
courted." In his profession, he had displayed "so much brilliancy," that up
and down the coast "people accepted him as a genius." Like James
Steerforth, the famous Dickens character, he possessed "rare and dangerous" qualities, among other things, being too bold and clever for his own
good. Given to "recklessness," he suffered from "weaknesses," including
hard drinking, wasteful spending, and probably womanizing. "Yet," the
writer concluded, "in his profession this solitary man had been a prince."[42]

NOTES

PROLOGUE

1. "Died in County Hospital," *Ventura Free Press,* March 4, 1904.
2. "Some Reminiscences of Leonard's Career," *Bakersfield Morning Echo,* March 10, 1904; "The Life Tragedy of J. W. Leonard," *Bakersfield Daily Californian,* March 19, 1904.

CHAPTER 1

1. Wilbur S. Shepperson, *Emigration and Disenchantment* (Norman: University of Oklahoma Press, 1965), pp. 6–7; Charlotte Erickson, "English," in *Harvard Encyclopedia of American Ethnic Groups,* ed. Stephen Thernstrom (Cambridge, Mass.: Harvard University Press, 1980), pp. 324–33; Charlotte Erickson, *Invisible Immigrants, The Adaptation of English and Scottish Immigrants in Nineteenth-Century America* (Coral Gables, Fla.: University of Miami Press, 1972), pp. 393–405; Charlotte Erickson, *Leaving England: Essays on British Emigration in the Nineteenth Century* (Ithaca, N.Y.: Cornell University Press, 1994), p. 25; Charlotte Erickson, *Invisible Immigrants* (London: London School of Economics and Political Science, n. d.), pp. 3–7; Dudley Baines, *Migration in a Mature Economy* (Cambridge: Cambridge University Press, 1985), pp. 9–11, 16–17, 23–27, 33–34; F. M. L. Thompson, *The Rise of Respectable Society: A Social History of Victorian Britain, 1830–1900* (Cambridge, Mass.: Harvard University Press, 1988), pp. 198–99, 202–203.
2. Erickson, "English," p. 326; Homer L. Kerr, "Migration into Texas, 1860–1880," *Southwestern Historical Quarterly* 70 (October 1966): 203; Ralph A. Wooster, "Foreigners in Principal Towns of Ante-Bellum Texas," *Southwestern Historical Quarterly* 65 (October 1962): 208–209. For a general discussion of English immigrants to Texas, see Thomas W. Cutrer, *The English Texans* (San Antonio: Institute of Texan Cultures, 1985).
3. Geoffrey Best, *Mid-Victorian Britain, 1851–1875* (New York: Schochen Books, 1972), pp. 7–9; Asa Briggs, *Victorian Cities* (New York: Harper and Row, 1963), pp. 323–28; Sally Mitchell, ed., *Victorian Britain* (New York: Garland Publishing, 1988), pp. 464–65; L. C. B. Seaman, *Life in Victorian London*

(London: B. T. Batsford, 1973), pp. 8–11; Thompson, *Rise of Respectable Society,* pp. 28–29.

4. John W. Leonard to Kate Mouton, June 20, 1932, author's collection (unless otherwise noted, all subsequent letters, papers, and diaries cited are from the author's manuscript collection). Among the seven Leonard children, only John, Hannah, and the eldest son, James, survived to adulthood. Thompson, *Rise of Respectable Society,* discusses the "respectable workingman," pp. 198–99, 202–203.

5. John W. Leonard, "John W. Leonard, 80, Writes His Own Story of First Enterprise," *Beaumont Enterprise,* August 3, 1930.

6. John W. Leonard, "Uncle Willie's Column," *Beaumont Enterprise,* December 23, 1928.

7. John W. Leonard, "Beaumont, Old and New," *Beaumont Enterprise,* January 30, 1927. Operations of the Mallory Line are discussed in James P. Baughman, "The Evolution of Rail-Water Systems of Transportation in the Gulf-Southwest, 1836–1890," *Journal of Southern History* 34 (August 1968): 364–67.

8. Leonard, "Beaumont, Old and New," January 30, 1927.

9. Ibid.

10. Leonard, "Beaumont, Old and New," January 27, 1930; W. T. Block, *Emerald of the Neches: The Chronicles of Beaumont, Texas, from Reconstruction to Spindletop* (Nederland, Tex.: W. T. Block, 1980), p. 265, cites a *Galveston Weekly News,* May 18, 1882, quotation of the *Orange Tribune,* in which Capt. J. Pederson, skipper of the *Silas,* reported that the oil pond, once "two miles in length," had "pretty nearly disappeared."

11. Leonard, "Beaumont, Old and New," January 30, 1927.

12. John W. Leonard to Kate Lamb Mouton, June 20, 1932; Leonard, "Uncle Willie's Column," August 12, 1928.

13. Leonard, "Uncle Willie's Column," August 12, 1928. Robert Leonard's first wife, Gertrude, died, and in 1868 he married Rosalie Patridge.

14. Leonard, "Uncle Willie's Column," January 6, 1929.

15. Census and Birth Records, Office of Population Census and Surveys (hereafter cited as OPCS), London. Both Will Johnson and John Leonard were known by family and friends as "Willie." And John Leonard used the name in later years in his "Uncle Willie's Columns." However, for purposes of clarity, the author limits the name's use to Will Johnson.

16. Census and Population Records, OPCS, London; E. B. Kelly, ed., *Post Office Directory of Norfolk* (Norwich, U.K.: Kelly and Company, 1858), pp. 222, 255–57; Paul Richards, *King's Lynn* (Chichester, U.K.: Phillimore, 1990), pp. xiii, 13–17, 32–36.

17. Paul Richards to Robert J. Robertson, January 27, 1995.

18. Kelly, ed., *Directory of Norfolk,* pp. 225–27; Richards, *King's Lynn,* pp. 112, 139–40, 152; Vera Perrott, *Victoria's Lynn, Boom & Prosperity* (Seaford, U.K.: Vista Books, 1995), pp. 8–10, 20–25; Thompson, *Rise of Respectable Society,* pp. 46–47.

19. Thomas Johnson's death was recorded in *Lynn Advertiser,* August 18, 1866.

20. Sarah Ann Johnson to Robert H. Leonard, June 11, 1869.

21. John W. Leonard was born June 6, 1849; Will Johnson, September 13, 1852. Census and Birth Records, OPCS, London.

22. J. W. L. Johnson to Samuel Johnson, November 3, 1870.

23. Sarah Ann Johnson to J. W. L. Johnson, September 1, 1869. For coverage of Alexandra dock opening, see *London Illustrated News,* July 17, 1869.

24. Sarah Ann Johnson to J. W. L. Johnson, September 1, 1869; J. W. L. Johnson to Samuel Johnson, May 20, 1870.

25. In all, there are thirty-three contemporary letters in the author's Leonard-Johnson-Lamb collection, beginning in 1869 and ending in 1932.

26. Leonard, "Uncle Willie's Column," January 6, 1929.

27. Leonard, "Beaumont, Old and New," January 30, 1927.

28. Robert J. Robertson, "Beaumont on the Eve of the Civil War, As Seen in *The Beaumont Banner,*" *Texas Gulf Historical and Biographical Record* 30 (November 1994): 8–26; Paul Isaac, "Beaumont, Texas," in *The New Handbook of Texas,* vol. 1, edited by Ron C. Tyler, et al. (Austin: Texas State Historical Association, 1996), p. 447.

29. Leonard, "Beaumont, Old and New," January 30, 1927; see also, Leonard, "Uncle Willie's Column," January 15, 1930.

30. Leonard, "Beaumont, Old and New," January 30, 1927; see also, Leonard, "Uncle Willie's Column," January 6, 1929.

31. Frederick Law Olmsted, *A Journey through Texas; or a Saddletrip on the Southwestern Frontier* (Austin: University of Texas Press, 1978), p. 376; W. T. Block, ed., "Beaumont in the 1850s: Excerpts from the Writings of Henry R. Green," *Texas Gulf Historical and Biographical Record* 11 (November 1975): 56; Leonard, "Uncle Willie's Column," January 15, 1930; see also Leonard, "Memories of Col. Averill," *Beaumont Enterprise,* date unknown.

32. Leonard, "Beaumont, Old and New," January 30, 1927.

33. Leonard, "Uncle Willie's Column," January 6, 1929.

34. Ibid.; the author could not locate Simmons or Watkins in the 1870 census.

35. Milton M. Gordon, *Assimilation in American Life* (New York: Oxford University Press, 1964), pp. 60–83, discusses the nature of assimilation, considering the process complete when the immigrant has acquired the language and the social ritual of the host community and can participate without prejudice in the common life, economic and political.

Chapter 2

1. J. W. L. Johnson to family, June 20, 1869.

2. T. J. Russell, "Pioneer Reminiscences of Jefferson County," *Beaumont Daily Journal,* February 4, 1906; John W. Leonard to Kate Lamb Mouton, June 20, 1932.

3. Randolph B. Campbell, "Statehood, Civil War, and Reconstruction, 1846–1876," in *Texas Through Time: Evolving Interpretations*, eds. Walter L. Buenger and Robert A. Calvert (College Station: Texas A&M University Press, 1991), p. 179; Frederick Eby, *The Development of Education in Texas* (New York: MacMillan, 1925), pp. 149–56; C. E. Evans, *The Story of Texas Schools* (Austin, Tex.: Steck Co., 1955), pp. 57–69, 72–77; Max Berger and Lee Wilborn, "Education," in *New Handbook of Texas*, vol. 2, pp. 788–94.

4. Alton Hornsby, Jr., "The Freedmen's Bureau Schools in Texas, 1865–1870," *Southwestern Historical Quarterly* 76 (April 1973): 397–99; Barry A. Crouch, *The Freedmen's Bureau and Black Texans* (Austin: University of Texas Press, 1992), pp. 59–67, 83–88, 128–29; William Richter, *Overreached on All Sides: The Freedmen's Bureau Administrators, 1865–1868* (College Station: Texas A&M University Press, 1991), pp. 231–35; James Smallwood, "Black Education in Reconstruction Texas: The Contributions of the Freedmen's Bureau and Benevolent Societies," *East Texas Historical Journal* 19 (spring 1981): 17–35; Anna Victoria Wilson, "Education for African Americans," in *New Handbook of Texas*, vol. 2, pp. 794–96.

5. Eby, *The Development of Education in Texas*, p. 157.

6. Clarke A. Mathews, "History of the Schools of Jefferson County to 1883" (master's thesis, University of Texas, 1937); W. T. Block, "Early Beaumont Education: Frontier Schools Provided the City's Leaders of the Future," unpublished MS, author's collection. The Freedmen's Bureau schools are discussed by Barry A. Crouch, "The Freedmen's Bureau in Beaumont," part two, *Texas Gulf Historical and Biographical Record* 29 (November 1993): 23–26.

7. Stanley James Curtis, *History of Education in Great Britain* (London: University Tutorial Press, 1953), pp. 207–208; John S. Hurt, *Education in Evolution: Church, State, Society and Popular Education, 1800–1870* (London: Rupert Hart-Davis, 1971), pp. 132–49.

8. Newcastle Commission, Report, 1858, showing the curriculum and signed by Charles William Croad, on file at The British and Foreign School Society Archives Centre, London.

9. J. W. L. Johnson to Samuel Johnson, November 3, 1870. The tenures of Croad and Samuel at the British School in King's Lynn are documented in Norfolk directories, 1858–69, on file in the Central Library, King's Lynn, Norfolk.

10. John William Adsman, *English Education, 1789–1902* (Cambridge: Cambridge University Press, 1930), pp. 25, 141–44; J. Dover Wilson, ed., *The Schools of England* (Chapel Hill: University of North Carolina Press, 1929), pp. 43–50; Hurt, *Education in Evolution*, pp. 14–19.

11. John W. Leonard to Kate Lamb Mouton, June 20, 1932; Leonard discusses his grades in his "Uncle Willie's Column," March 24, 1929.

12. Leonard, "Uncle Willie's Column," September 9, 1928. Hannah Leonard Lamb's reading habits are discussed in chapter 2. The Victorian culture of books

and reading is discussed by Richard D. Altick, *Victorian People and Ideas* (New York: W. W. Norton, 1973), pp. 5-6, 17-18, 59-63, 247-55; Best, *Mid-Victorian Britain,* pp. 170, 225-27; Asa Briggs, *A Social History of England* (New York: Viking Press, 1983), p. 229; and Thompson, *Rise of Respectable Society,* pp. 139-41, explains "that the school-going habit had become deeply rooted in the working classes."

13. John W. Leonard, "Five Decades Ago in Beaumont," *Beaumont Enterprise,* February 6, 1927.

14. Ibid.

15. Ibid.

16. J. W. L. Johnson to family, June 20, 1869.

17. Leonard, "Five Decades Ago in Beaumont."

18. Ibid.

19. Ibid.

20. Ibid.

21. Ibid.

22. Ibid.

23. Stewart D. Smith, "Schools and Schoolmen: Chapters in Texas Education," (Ph.D. diss., North Texas State University, 1974), pp. 44-45, 155-56, 300-302.

24. J. W. L. Johnson to family, December 15, 1869.

25. Ibid.; Robert H. Leonard to J. W. L. Johnson, February 22, 1870.

26. J. W. L. Johnson to Sarah Ann Johnson, July, 1870.

27. Carl H. Moneyhon, "Public Education and Texas Reconstruction Politics, 1871-1874," *Southwestern Historical Quarterly* 94 (January 1989): 393-416; Smith, "Schools and Schoolmen," pp. 10-23; Max Berger and Lee Wilborn, "Education," in *New Handbook of Texas,* vol. 2, pp. 788-94; also in the *New Handbook,* see Moneyhon, "Reconstruction," vol. 5, pp. 474-81.

28. Smith, "Schools and Schoolmen," pp. 22-24.

29. Leonard, "Five Decades Ago in Beaumont." *Steele's* and other textbooks prescribed by the Davis administration are discussed by Michael Allen White, "History of Education in Texas, 1860-1884" (Ed.D. diss., Baylor University, 1969), pp. 197-99.

30. Leonard, "Five Decades Ago in Beaumont."

31. *Beaumont News Beacon,* April 19, 1873; Smith, "Schools and Schoolmen," pp. 22-25; Patrick George Williams, "Redeemer Democrats and the Roots of Modern Texas, 1872-1884" (Ph.D. diss., Columbia University, 1996), pp. 40-45.

32. Leonard, "Uncle Willie's Column," September 16, 1928. Olivia Rigsby's school is described in Clarke A. Mathews, "History of the Schools of Jefferson County to 1883," pp. 107-108. The *Neches Valley News,* January 7, 1871, carried an advertisement showing the offerings of Mrs. A. E. Lynch's school: "Educational. Mrs. A. E. Lynch returns thanks to the citizens of Beaumont and vicinity, for the liberal patronage bestowed, and hopes by care and attention to merit the confidence

of Patron and pupil. The first term for 1871 will commence January 2nd, and continue six months. Terms of Tuition: Payable Monthly, in Specie. Spelling $ 2.00. Reading, writing, geography, arithmetic, grammar . . . $ 2.50. Higher branches . . . $3.00. No deduction for absence, unless in case of protracted illness."

33. J. W. L. Johnson to Samuel Johnson, May 24, 1870. The school operated by Will and Mrs. Neyland is mentioned in the *Jasper News Boy,* May 7, 1870.

34. J. W. L. Johnson to Samuel Johnson, May 24, 1870.

35. John W. Leonard to J. W. L. Johnson, September 17, 1870; February 14, 1871.

36. J. W. L. Johnson to family, December 15, 1869. In "Beaumont, Old and New," January 30, 1927, John reports that he was treated for malaria in Beaumont by Dr. Simmons, "a physician of the old school," who, like other practitioners of the period, prescribed "bitter 10-grain doses" of quinine and "drastic blue-mass pills as big as common marbles." See also Leonard, "Uncle Willie's Column," March 10, 1929: When John's ailment took chronic form, Dr. Simmons administered another common remedy— Towler's solution of arsenic followed by its antidote, tincture of iron.

37. J. W. L. Johnson to Sarah Ann Johnson, November 27, 1870.

38. John W. Leonard to Sarah Ann Johnson, July 22, 1870; February 6, 1871.

39. J. W. L. Johnson to family, December 15, 1869.

40. John W. Leonard to Sarah Ann Johnson, July 22, December 6, 1870.

41. Leonard, "Beaumont, Old and New," January 30, 1927.

42. Ibid.

43. J. W. L. Johnson to Sara Ann Johnson, November 27, 1870.

44. J. W. L. Johnson to Sarah Ann Johnson, August 3, 1871.

45. J. W. L. Johnson to Sarah Ann Johnson, May 24, 1870; John W. Leonard to Sarah Ann Johnson, February 6, 1871.

46. *Beaumont News Beacon,* April 12, 19; May 3, 31, 1873.

47. J. W. L. Johnson to Sarah Ann Johnson, December 1, 1874; Mathews, "History of the Schools in Jefferson County to 1883," pp. 108–16.

48. Leonard, "Uncle Willie's Column," February 16, 19??.

49. Hannah Leonard Lamb, diary, May 1870-April 1874.

50. Ibid.

51. Ibid.

52. Ibid. Victorian reading habits are discussed by Altick, *Victorian People and Ideas,* pp. 5–6, 17–18, 59–63, 247–55; Best, *Mid-Victorian Britain,* pp. 170, 225–27; Briggs, *A Social History,* p. 229.

53. Hannah Leonard Lamb, diary, May 1870-April 1874.

54. J. W. L. Johnson to Sarah Ann Johnson, October 10, 1877.

55. *Beaumont Lumberman,* June 21, 1878. Promising "An English education" was a ploy used commonly in private school advertisements: see advertisement for Mary A. Browne's Young Ladies Day School in Houston, *Houston Telegraph,* Au-

gust 16, 1870; also, for Professor T. J. Giradeau's English and Classical School for Boys in Galveston, *Galveston Daily News,* August 24, 1872; and in the same paper, Mrs. Sylvanus Reed's Boarding School for Young Ladies in New York. "An English education" probably carried two connotations: one meaning derived from the English system; the other simply denoting basic courses—reading, writing, arithmetic, and English grammar. See Frederick Eby, *Education in Texas, Source Materials* (Austin: University of Texas Bulletin, 1918), p. 337; also, Anita Louise White, "The Teacher in Texas: 1836–1879" (Ed.D diss., Baylor University, 1972), pp. 126, 759.

CHAPTER 3

1. Leonard, "Beaumont, Old and New," January 30, 1927.

2. J. W. L. Johnson to Sarah Ann Johnson, November 27, 1870.

3. For elaboration on the social, cultural, and political roles lawyers played in Texas during this period, see Ralph A. Wooster, *The Secession Conventions of the South* (Princeton, N.J.: Princeton University Press, 1962), pp. 3–5, 126, 258; Randolph B. Campbell and Richard G. Lowe, *Wealth and Power in Antebellum Texas* (College Station: Texas A&M University Press, 1977), pp. 58, 94, 121; Mary Helen Hatchell Freeman, "East Texas, A Social and Economic History of the Counties East of the Trinity River, 1850–1860" (master's thesis, Lamar University, 1976), pp. 93–95; Ralph W. Yarbrough, "A History of Law Licensing in Texas," in *Centennial History of the Texas Bar,* ed. Traylor Russell (Austin, Tex.: Eakin Press, 1981), pp. 181–84; Judith Linsley and Ellen Rienstra, "O'Brien, George Washington," in *New Handbook of Texas,* vol. 4, p. 1098. The rise of English men from working class families to the ranks of white collar workers is discussed in Erickson, *Invisible Immigrants,* pp. 394–97.

4. Leonard, "Uncle Willie's Column," August 12, 1928.

5. Ibid., January 1, 1932.

6. Leonard, "Uncle Willie's Column," August 12, 1928.

7. Ibid., October 12, 1930.

8. J. W. L. Johnson to Samuel Johnson, November 3, 1870; J. W. L. Johnson to Sarah Ann Johnson, August 3, 1871.

9. Leonard, "Beaumont, Old and New," January 30, 1927; Robert Wooster, "James Armstrong," in *New Handbook of Texas,* vol. 1, pp. 243–44; *Biographical Directory of Texas Conventions and Congresses, 1832–1845* (1845; reprint, St. Augustine, Tex.: S. Malone, 1986), p. 44; Leonard, "Uncle Willie's Column," August 12, 1928.

10. Leonard, "Uncle Willie's Column," October 12, 1930; Nancy Jo Newton and Frank Newton, "Legal Education in Texas," in *Centennial History of the Texas Bar,* ed. Traylor Russell (Austin, Tex.: Eakin Press, 1981), pp. 159–62; Joseph W. McKnight, "Law Schools," in *New Handbook of Texas,* vol. 4, p. 122.

11. Gerald Ashford, "Jacksonian Liberalism and Spanish Law in Early Texas," *Southwestern Historical Quarterly* 57 (July 1953): 1–37; N. J. Newton and F. Newton, "Legal Education in Texas," p. 159; Spurgeon E. Bell, "A History of the Texas Courts," in *Centennial History of the Texas Bar,* ed. Traylor Russell (Austin, Tex.: Eakin Press, 1981), p. 194–95; Yarbrough, "A History of Law Licensing in Texas," p. 184; Edward L. Markham, "Reception of the Common Law of England in Texas and Judicial Attitudes toward That Reception, 1840–1859," *Texas Law Review* 29 (1952): 904, 908–10.

12. Leonard, "Five Decades Ago in Beaumont"; Leonard, "Uncle Willie's Column," August 5, 1928.

13. Leonard, "Five Decades Ago in Beaumont."

14. Leonard, "Uncle Willie's Column," January 30, 1927, December 27, 1931.

15. J. W. L. Johnson to Sarah Ann Johnson, July 1870; J. W. L. Johnson to Samuel Johnson, November 3, 1870.

16. J. W. L. Johnson to Samuel Johnson, November 3, 1870.

17. Leonard, "Uncle Willie's Column," August 12, 1928; Bell, "A History of the Texas Courts," pp. 197–99; Yarbrough, "A History of the Law Licensing in Texas," p. 183.

18. Jefferson County District Court minutes, November 24, 1870, Jefferson County Courthouse, Beaumont, Tex.; Leonard, "Uncle Willie's Column," August 12, 1928.

19. Copy of original license dated November 24, 1870. Original document in possession of Howard E. Tompkins.

20. Jefferson County District Court minutes, November 24, 1870.

21. John W. Leonard to Sarah Ann Johnson, December 6, 1870; Jefferson County District Court minutes, December 3, 1870, Jefferson County Courthouse, Beaumont, Tex. Leonard identified Willard as an African American in "Five Decades Ago in Beaumont"; McDaniel is listed as black in *United States Tenth Census, 1880,* manuscript returns, microfilm copies, Tyrrell Historical Library, Beaumont, Tex.

22. Jefferson County District Court minutes, December 3, 1870.

23. Leonard, "Five Decades Ago in Beaumont."

24. Jefferson County District Court minutes, December 3, 1870; Randolph B. Campbell, *A Southern Community in Crisis: Harrison County, Texas, 1850–1880* (Austin: Texas State Historical Association, 1983), p. 131.

25. Leonard, "Five Decades ago in Beaumont." J. D. Tarver is listed in *United States Ninth Census, 1870,* Hardin County, Tex., #459.

26. Leonard, "Five Decades Ago in Beaumont."

27. Leonard, "Uncle Willie's Column," October 12, 1930; Bentley and Pilgrim [law firm], ed., *Texas Legal Directory* (Austin, Tex.: Democratic Statesman Office, 1877), pp. 20–22, 63. The first district also included Chambers, Jasper, Liberty, Newton, Polk, San Jacinto, and Tyler Counties.

28. Leonard, "Uncle Willie's Column," October 12, 1930.

29. Ibid.; August 5, 1928.

30. John W. Leonard to Sarah Ann Johnson, February 6, 1871.

31. James I. Rock and W. I. Smith, *Southern and Western Texas, 1878,* (St. Louis, Mo.: A. H. Granger, 1878), pp. 78–80, quoted in Robert L. Schaadt, *The History of Hardin County* (Kountze, Tex.: Hardin County Historical Commission, 1991), pp. 24–28; Patricia L. Duncan, "Hardin County," in *New Handbook of Texas,* vol. 3, pp. 457–58.

32. *United States Ninth Census, 1870,* Hardin County, Tex., show only twenty-eight residents (2 percent) born outside the former Confederacy; see household #457 for Hannah Arline; Schaadt, *History of Hardin County,* p. 27.

33. Leonard, "Five Decades Ago in Beaumont"; Schaadt, *History of Hardin County,* p. 27.

34. Leonard, "Uncle Willie's Column," February 6, 1927.

35. Ibid.; August 13, 1928. For a biography of Kirby, see Mary Lasswell, *John Henry Kirby: Prince of the Pines* (Austin, Tex.: Encino Press, 1967).

36. Jefferson County District Court minutes, 1871–72, pp. 47, 65.

37. Schaadt, *History of Hardin County,* pp. 24–25; Leonard, "Uncle Willie's Column," September 23, 1928.

38. John W. Leonard to J. W. L. Johnson, September 17, 1870.

39. John W. Leonard to Sarah Ann Johnson, December 16, 1870; February 6, 1871.

40. John W. Leonard to J. W. L. Johnson, February 14, 1871.

41. *United States Ninth Census, 1870,* Hardin County, Tex., household #466.

42. "Marriage Records," *Yellowed Pages* (Southeast Texas Genealogical and Historical Society, Beaumont) 5, no. 3 (August 1975): 129.

43. *State of Texas against William Chambers, Judge First Judicial District, before the Senate of the Fourteenth Legislature, Sitting as a High Court of Impeachment* (Austin: Cardwell and Walker, 1874), pp. 1–129. Records of the impeachment proceedings set forth details of the 1871 Jacob Luder estate, the 1873 trial of *Texas v. Leonard,* and related events; included are various direct quotations by the participants.

44. Ibid.

45. Ibid.

46. Ibid.

47. Ibid.

48. Ibid.

49. Hardin County District Court minutes index, Kountze, Tex.; *United States Tenth Census, 1880,* manuscript returns, Tyler County, Tex., #179.

50. *United States Ninth Census, 1870,* manuscript returns; advertisement (dated July 27, 1872), *Beaumont News-Beacon,* January 18, 1873; J. W. L. Johnson to Sarah Ann Johnson, July 1–26, 1872; *Neches Valley News,* July 27, 1872.

51. Leonard, "Beaumont, Old and New," January 30, 1927.
52. Ibid.

CHAPTER 4

1. J. W. L. Johnson to Samuel Johnson, November 3, 1870.
2. Ibid.
3. Billy D. Ledbetter, "White Texans' Attitudes toward the Political Equality of Negroes, 1865-1870," *Phylon* 40 (September 1979): 253-63.
4. Carl H. Moneyhon, "Reconstruction," pp. 474-81. From the viewpoint of historians, the Reconstruction era has been controversial and has received a variety of interpretations, ranging from the "traditional," which praises the Democrats and vilifies the Republicans, to the "revisionist," which tends toward an opposite position from that of the traditionalists. For a discussion of this historiography, see Campbell, "Statehood, Civil War, and Reconstruction," pp. 191-96; Ralph A. Wooster, "The Civil War and Reconstruction in Texas," in *A Guide to the History of Texas,* eds. Light T. Cummins and Alvin R. Bailey, Jr. (New York: Greenwood Press, 1988), pp. 44-50; and Eric Foner, *Reconstruction, America's Unfinished Revolution, 1863-1877* (New York: Harper and Row, 1988), pp. xix-xxvii. In this history, the author has not produced a complete or fully balanced version of Texas Reconstruction politics; he has not devoted sufficient attention to the aspirations and activities of Texas Republicans, especially black Republicans. Instead, he has concentrated on Will Johnson and John Leonard, outlining their political and racial attitudes, their solidarity with conservative white Democrats, and their efforts to help the Democratic Party regain control of the state.
5. Leonard, "Five Decades Ago in Beaumont."
6. David H. Donald, "Reconstruction, 1865-1877," in *The New Encyclopedia Britannica,* vol. 29 (1990), pp. 237-40; Randolph B. Campbell, "Grass Roots Reconstruction in Texas: An Overview," unpublished MS, author's collection, pp. 7-8; for "black codes," see Barry A. Crouch, "All the Vile Passions: The Texas Black Code of 1866," *Southwestern Historical Quarterly* 97 (July 1993): 13-15, 32-34; and Eric Foner, *Reconstruction, America's Unfinished Revolution, 1863-1877* (New York: Harper and Row, 1988), pp. 198-202.
7. Donald, "Reconstruction," pp. 237-40; Foner, *Reconstruction,* pp. 228-71; William L. Richter, *The Army in Texas During Reconstruction, 1865-1870* (College Station: Texas A&M University Press, 1987), pp. 187-96. The imposition of the "iron clad" oath and removal of officials is discussed by Moneyhon, "Reconstruction," pp. 474-81; Campbell, "Grass Roots Reconstruction," p. 9, explains that the "iron clad" oath required a person to swear that he had never sworn loyalty to the United States and subsequently given aid and comfort to the Confederacy. Campbell recaps the 1967 voter registration, showing that about 49,000 blacks and

59,000 whites were enrolled, with 7,500-12,000 former Confederates being disfranchised (p. 10).

8. Alwyn Barr, *Reconstruction to Reform, Texas Politics, 1876-1906* (Austin: University of Texas Press, 1971), pp. 7-8; Moneyhon, "Reconstruction," pp. 474-81, discusses the wholesale removal of local officials who could not pass the "iron clad" oath.

9. Randolph B. Campbell, "Reconstruction in Jefferson County, 1865-1876," *Texas Gulf Historical and Biographical Record* 31 (November 1995): 13-14.

10. Ibid.

11. Ibid.; Williams, "Redeemer Democrats," p. 18, describes Texas Redeemers as "a varied cohort," representing business, planting, and railroad interests, and including men—such as Richard Coke, Richard Hubbard, Ashbel Smith, William P. Ballinger, and Benjamin Epperson—varied in their economic and political interests but united by their common dislike of the Reconstruction regime.

12. Campbell, "Reconstruction in Jefferson County," pp. 10-11; Robertson, "Beaumont on the Eve of the Civil War," pp. 8-22.

13. Campbell, "Reconstruction in Jefferson County," pp. 10-11; Robert J. Robertson, "Slavery and the Coming of the Civil War, As Seen in *The Beaumont Banner*," *East Texas Historical Journal* 34, no. 1 (spring 1996): 14-29. O'Brien's military service is recorded in Cooper K. Ragan, ed., "The Diary of Captain O'Brien, 1863," *Southwestern Historical Quarterly* 67 (July 1963); Fletcher's military service is recounted in William A. Fletcher, *Rebel Private: Front and Rear* (New York: Dutton, 1995)

14. *United States Eighth Census, 1860,* manuscript returns, shows #291, Robert Leonard, lawyer with $500 real property and $100 personal property; Leonard's military service is recorded in Harold B. Simpson, *Hood's Texas Brigade: A Compendium* (Hillsboro, Tex.: Hill Jr. College Series, 1977), p. 211; for military records, see also Company Muster Rolls, Company F, 5th Regiment, Texas Infantry, Confederate Research Center, Hillsboro, Tex. Leonard, "Uncle Willie's Column," August 12, 1928, claims that Robert Leonard also served as a provost marshal in Shreveport, Louisiana, but the author was unable to confirm this information.

15. Robert Wooster, "Armstrong, James," in *New Handbook of Texas,* vol. 1, pp. 243-44; Charles W. Ramsdell, *Reconstruction in Texas* (New York: Columbia University, 1910), pp. 200-201, identifies Armstrong and Lemuel D. Evans as conservative leaders at the 1868-69 Constitutional Convention.

16. Leonard, "Uncle Willie's Column," August 5, 1928.

17. Randolph B. Campbell, "George W. Whitmore: East Texas Unionist," *East Texas Historical Journal* 28, no. 1 (spring 1990): 17-28; Campbell, "Whitmore, George Washington," in *New Handbook of Texas,* vol. 6, p. 948. An estimated 7,500-10,000 Confederates were disfranchised statewide, according to William R.

Russ, Jr., in "Radical Disfranchisement in Texas, 1867–1870," *Southwestern Historical Quarterly* 38 (July 1934), pp. 40–52.

18. Leonard, "Five Decades Ago in Beaumont."

19. David Cresap Moore, *The Politics of Deference: A Study of the Mid-Nineteenth English Political System* (New York: Harvester Press, 1976), pp. 246–47, 371–74, 386–90; 1869 Tex Const, Art VI, sec 1–2; Ralph A. Wooster, *People in Power, Courthouse and Statehouse in the Lower South, 1850–1860* (Knoxville: University of Tennessee Press, 1969), p. 25.

20. John P. Carrier, "A Political History of Texas during the Reconstruction, 1867–1874" (Ph.D. diss., Vanderbilt University, 1971), pp. 394–404.

21. Carl H. Moneyhon, *Republicanism in Reconstruction Texas* (Austin: University of Texas Press, 1980), pp. 122–24; Moneyhon, "Davis, Edmund Jackson," in *New Handbook of Texas*, vol. 2, pp. 525–27.

22. Campbell, "Reconstruction in Jefferson County," pp. 16, 26–27.

23. Moneyhon, *Republicanism in Reconstruction Texas*, pp. 122–24; Carrier, "Political History of Texas," pp. 394–95; Williams, "Redeemer Democrats," pp. 20–28; Foner, *Reconstruction*, xxv, observes that "black participation in Southern public life after 1867 was the most radical development of the Reconstruction years, a massive experiment in interracial democracy without precedent."

24. Carrier, "Political History of Texas," pp. 476–81; Moneyhon, *Republicanism in Reconstruction Texas*, p. 134; Chandler Davidson, "African Americans," in *New Handbook of Texas*, vol. 1, pp. 46–51; African American leaders are discussed by J. Mason Brewer, *Negro Legislators of Texas* (Austin: Jenkins Publishing Co., 1970). Texas women did not win full voting rights until 1919.

25. Donald, "Reconstruction," pp. 237–39; Ledbetter, "White Texans' Attitudes," pp. 253–63; Barry A. Crouch and Leon J. Schultz, "Crisis in Color: Racial Separation in Texas during Reconstruction," *Civil War History* 16 (March 1970): 39–49; Barry A. Crouch, "Hidden Sources of Black History: The Texas Freedmen's Bureau Records as a Case Study," *Southwestern Historical Quarterly* 83 (January 1980): 214–16, 222–24; Richter, *Overreached on All Sides*, p. 293.

26. Campbell, "Reconstruction in Jefferson County," pp. 15, 17, 23, 25.

27. Barry A. Crouch, "The Freedmen's Bureau in Beaumont," part one, *Texas Gulf Historical and Biographical Record* 28 (1992): 12–14.

28. Derek Beales, *From Castlereagh to Gladstone, 1815–1885* (New York: Norton, 1969), pp. 174, 218–19, 223, 284; racial prejudice against black Africans during the nineteenth century is revealed in "Negro" in *Encyclopedia Britannica*, 9th ed., pp. 325–28; W. L. Burn, *The Age of Equipoise: A Study of the Mid-Victorian Generation* (London: George Allen and Unwin, 1964), p. 85; Walter E. Houghton, *The Victorian Frame of Mind* (New Haven, Conn.: Yale University Press, 1957), pp. 212–13; Christine Bolt, *Victorian Attitudes to Race* (London: Routledge and Kegan Paul, 1971), pp. ix–xii, 29–74, 78, 105, 133. Bolt employs journals, newspapers, books, and documents to construct "a comparative survey of the most characteristic Victorian

opinions about the colored races" (pp. x-xiii). According to Bolt, Victorians were al-most unanimously opposed to the enfranchisement of Southern blacks, and the Vic-torian's "hostility was directed not merely against the American freedman, but against the African generally" (p. 74). An example of this racial attitude, Bolt argues, is found among the British missionaries in Africa: "The sense of spiritual superiority . . . was in Africa easily transformed into a feeling of racial superiority, because of the enor-mous barriers existing between Europeans and Africans in terms of color, habitat, in-dustrial achievement and social achievement, as well as religion" (p. 111). An inter-esting contrast to majority Victorian racial views can be found in the work of Georges Clemenceau, the young liberal Parisian newspaper correspondent who lived in the United States during 1865-70 and covered the Reconstruction story; he favored the concept of racial equality and endorsed African American suffrage. Clemenceau, *American Reconstruction, 1865-1870*, ed. Fernand Baldensperger (New York: Lin-coln MacVeigh-The Dial Press, 1928), pp. 22-24, 33-39, 62-63, 65, 92.

29. Cutrer, *English Texans*, pp. 83-91.

30. Leonard, "Uncle Willie's Column," January 6, 1929.

31. Democrats often used the term "carpetbagger" carelessly, applying it to all Republicans and dismissing them as outsiders. But this was a misnomer; among Governor Davis and the principal Republicans in his administration and in the leg-islature and judiciary, less than 15 percent actually fit the definition, "a person born in the North who moved to the South after 1865 and became involved in politics when Congress took over the process in 1867". See, Randolph B. Campbell, "Car-petbagger Rule in Reconstruction Texas: An Enduring Myth," *Southwestern His-torical Quarterly* 97 (April 1994): 587-96.

32. Moneyhon, *Republicanism in Reconstruction Texas*, pp. 126-28; Money-hon, "Reconstruction," in *New Handbook of Texas*, vol. 5, pp. 474-81.

33. Moneyhon, *Republicanism in Reconstruction Texas*, pp. 129-51; Money-hon, "Reconstruction," pp. 474-81; Campbell, "Grass Roots Reconstruction"; W. C. Nunn, *Texas under the Carpetbaggers* (Austin: University of Texas Press, 1962), pp. 43-92.

34. Alwyn Barr, *Black Texans: A History of Negroes in Texas, 1528-1971* (Austin, Tex.: Jenkins Publishing Co., 1982), pp. 43-49; Carrier, "Political History of Texas," pp. 448-51; Barry A. Crouch, "Guardian of the Freedpeople: Texas Freedmen's Bureau Agents and the Black Community," *Southern Studies* 3 (fall 1992): 195; Barry A. Crouch, *Freedmen's Bureau*, pp. 91-131; James Smallwood, *Time of Hope, Time of Despair, Black Texans during Reconstruction* (Port Wash-ington, N.Y.: Kennikat Press, 1981), pp. 134, 147, 150, 160; Williams, "Redeemer Democrats," pp. 33-38, is quoted in the text.

35. Carrier, "Political History of Texas," pp. 448-49.

36. Leonard, "Five Decades Ago in Beaumont."

37. Moneyhon, *Republicanism in Reconstruction Texas*, pp. 140-46; Williams, "Redeemer Democrats," p. 51, explains that the Democrats favored decentraliza-

tion, local self-government, and the elective principle and railed against Governor Davis's appointive powers.

38. Campbell, "Reconstruction in Jefferson County," p. 18.

39. Ibid.

40. Julianne Johnston and Robert Wooster, "Chambers, William Morton," in *New Handbook of Texas,* vol. 2, pp. 31–32.

41. Leonard, "Five Decades Ago in Beaumont."

42. Campbell, "Reconstruction in Jefferson County," p. 21.

43. Moneyhon, *Republicanism in Reconstruction Texas,* pp. 152–55; Nancy Beck Young, "Democratic Party," in *New Handbook of Texas,* vol. 2, pp. 586–90.

44. *Neches Valley News,* January 7, 1871.

45. "Loyal League Hunter," *Neches Valley News,* August 20, 1870.

46. *Neches Valley News,* January 7, 1871.

47. Ibid., May 27, 1871.

48. Ibid.

49. Ibid.

50. Ibid.

51. Ibid.

52. Moneyhon, *Republicanism in Reconstruction Texas,* pp. 152–55; Thomas Cutrer, "Herndon, William S.," in *New Handbook of Texas,* vol. 3, pp. 574–75; Carrier, "Political History of Texas," pp. 491–93; Williams, "Redeemer Democrats," p. 30–31.

53. *Neches Valley News,* May 27, 1871. With respect to the influence of "Eastern fanatics," Campbell, "Carpetbagger Rule," p. 590, demonstrates that the actual number of true "carpetbaggers" in Texas government was small.

54. Campbell, "Reconstruction in Jefferson County," p. 20.

55. Leonard, "Five Decades Ago in Beaumont."

56. Ibid.

57. Campbell, "Reconstruction in Jefferson County," p. 20; Moneyhon, *Republicanism in Reconstruction Texas,* p. 164; Carrier, "Political History of Texas," pp. 492–93.

58. Leonard, "Five Decades Ago in Beaumont."

CHAPTER 5

1. Campbell, "Reconstruction in Jefferson County," p. 8.

2. *Neches Valley News,* July 27, 1872.

3. Ibid.

4. Ibid.

5. J. W. L. Johnson to Sarah Ann Johnson, February ?, 1872.

6. J. W. L. Johnson to Sarah Ann Johnson, May 26, 1872.

7. J. W. L. Johnson to Sarah Ann Johnson, May 18, 1872.

8. *Neches Valley News,* July 27, 1872.

9. J. W. L. Johnson to Sarah Ann Johnson, July 1, 1872.

10. J. W. L. Johnson to Sarah Ann Johnson, February ?, April 26, 1872.

11. J. W. L. Johnson to Sarah Ann Johnson, April 26, 1872. Frederick Ogden and his sons, Lemuel P. and Ed C., are mentioned in Judith Walker Linsley and Ellen Walker Rienstra, *Beaumont: A Chronicle of Promise* (Woodland Hills, Calif.: Windsor Publications, 1982), 34, 37, 42, 123. Robert Wooster, "Ogden, Frederick W.," in *New Handbook of Texas,* vol. 4, p. 1114.

12. J. W. L. Johnson to Sarah Ann Johnson, May 18–26, 1872.

13. Ibid.

14. J. W. L. Johnson to Sarah Ann Johnson, July 1, 1872.

15. Ibid.; Will also ordered English literary magazines—*Punch, Judy,* and *Tomahawk*—for his own enjoyment and, no doubt, shared them with Viola and other friends. J. W. L. Johnson to Sarah Ann Johnson, May 18, 1872.

16. J. W. L. Johnson to Sarah Ann Johnson, September 20, 1872.

17. *Neches Valley News,* October 26, 1872. Carrier, "Political History of Texas," p. 503, discusses declining use of the racial issue.

18. *Neches Valley News,* October 26, 1872.

19. Leonard, "Five Decades Ago in Beaumont."

20. Carrier, "Political History of Texas," p. 500; Moneyhon, *Republicanism in Reconstruction Texas,* pp. 177–78. John later reported that, while having dinner with Watkins on the porch of a local hotel, they witnessed a horrific event: a black waiter who was carrying food near their table was struck dead by lightning. See, Leonard, "Five Decades Ago in Beaumont"; Leonard, "Uncle Willie's Column," May 27, 1928.

21. Carrier, "Political History of Texas," pp. 500–501; Nancy Beck Young, "Democratic Party," in *New Handbook of Texas,* vol. 2, pp. 586–90.

22. Carrier, "Political History of Texas," p. 502; Leonard, "Uncle Willie's Column," February 26, 1927.

23. Carrier, "Political History of Texas," pp. 500–501; Moneyhon, *Republicanism in Reconstruction Texas,* pp. 175–77; Leonard, "Uncle Willie's Column," May 27, 1928.

24. Leonard, "Uncle Willie's Column," May 27, 1928.

25. *Neches Valley News,* July 27, 1872.

26. Ibid.

27. *Neches Valley News,* October 26, 1872. For other contemporary accounts of the event, see *Galveston Daily News,* October 22, 25, 1872; *Galveston News,* October 23, 1872; *Houston Telegraph,* October 31, 1872. The author could not locate "L. D. Miller" in the U.S. censuses (manuscript returns) for 1870 and 1880. Democratic recruitment of African American speakers and voters is discussed by James Alex Baggett, "The Rise and Fall of the Texas Radicals, 1867–1883" (Ph.D. diss., North Texas State University, 1972), p. 188.

28. *Galveston Daily News,* October 25, 1872.

29. *Neches Valley News,* October 26, 1872.

30. Ibid., July 27, 1872.

31. Leonard, "Uncle Willie's Column," May 27, 1928.

32. Carrier, "Political History of Texas," pp. 469-70, 505-507, discusses increasing white immigration to Texas and the changing electorate; see also, Williams, "Redeemer Democrats," pp. 6, 30, 60.

33. Carrier, "Political History of Texas," pp. 505-507; Baggett, "Rise and Fall," pp. 189-90; Moneyhon, *Republicanism in Reconstruction Texas,* pp. 181-82.

34. Carrier, "Political History of Texas," pp. 507-509; Williams, "Redeemer Democrats," pp. 31-32, 35.

35. Carrier, "Political History of Texas," pp. 507-509; Williams, "Redeemer Democrats," pp. 31-32, 35; Campbell, "Grass Roots Reconstruction," p. 23.

36. Baggett, "Rise and Fall," p. 191; *Beaumont News-Beacon,* May 3, 1873, which included a reprint of an article from the *Galveston Daily News.* Williams, "Redeemer Democrats," pp. 64-85, explains that after "redeeming" the legislature and governorship, the Democrats turned their attention to the Republican judiciary and to certain counties controlled by black Republican majorities.

37. *Beaumont News-Beacon,* May 3, 1873.

38. Campbell, "Reconstruction in Jefferson County," p. 21; John W. Leonard to Robert H. Leonard, 1874, date unknown. *State of Texas against William Chambers,* pp. 1-129; Williams, "Redeemer Democrats," pp. 85-112.

39. *Beaumont News-Beacon,* August 29, 1873.

40. Ibid.

41. Ibid.

42. Ibid.

43. Ibid.

44. Ibid.

45. Carrier, "Political History of Texas," pp. 511-13; John W. Payne, "Coke, Richard," in *New Handbook of Texas,* vol. 2, p. 193; Cary D. Wintz, *Texas Politics in the Gilded Age, 1873-1890* (Boston: American Press, 1983), pp. 8-10.

46. Carrier, "Political History of Texas," pp. 513-15; Nunn, *Texas under the Carpetbaggers,* p. 118; Moneyhon, *Republicanism in Reconstruction Texas,* pp. 183-92.

47. Baggett, "Rise and Fall," p. 197; Carrier, "Political History of Texas," p. 519; Moneyhon, *Republicanism in Reconstruction Texas,* p. 191; Foner, *Reconstruction,* p. 549, remarks on white immigration and the inevitable results of the election.

48. Campbell, "Reconstruction in Jefferson County," pp. 22-23.

49. Carrier, "Political History of Texas," p. 520, discusses the election results and cites the headline of the *Galveston Daily News,* December 4, 1873.

CHAPTER 6

1. J. W. L. Johnson to Sarah Ann Johnson, July 1, 1872; Best, *Mid-Victorian Britain*, pp. 277-78; Houghton, *The Victorian Frame of Mind*, pp. 341-53; Seaman, *Life in Victorian London*, p. 121; Thompson, *Rise of Respectable Society*, pp. 51-113, discusses marriage, family, and birth control.

2. J. W. L. Johnson to Sarah Ann Johnson, September 20, 1872.

3. J. W. L. Johnson to Viola Ogden, March 19-20, 1873.

4. Ibid.; Vashti is also a figure in the Old Testament Book of Esther (1:10-19); the proud and beautiful queen of King Ahasuerus, she refused the King's instructions to display her beauty before his guests and was divorced.

5. Will would not turn age twenty-one until September 13, 1873.

6. *United States Tenth Census, 1880*, manuscript returns, household #543; *Men of Texas* (Houston, Tex.: Houston Post, 1903), pp. 1082-83.

7. Jefferson County marriage records, Jefferson County Courthouse, Beaumont, Tex.

8. Block, *Emerald of the Neches*, pp. 109, 120, cites *Galveston Daily News*, October 23, 1877, and May 3, 1878, which mention Johnson as "the *Lumberman* reporter."

9. The naturalization process was established under a series of federal laws, including the naturalization statutes of 1790, 1824, and 1870; naturalization was restricted to "free white males" until 1870, when new statutes decreed that "the naturalization laws are hereby extended to aliens of African nativity and to persons of African descent." James H. Kettner, *The Development of American Citizenship, 1608-1870* (Chapel Hill: University of North Carolina Press, 1978), p. 345; Frank George Franklin, *The Legislative History of Naturalization in the United States* (New York: Arno Press, 1969), p. 175.

10. Jefferson County District Court minutes, November 22, 1873, p. 172.

11. Margaret E. Hall, *How to Become a Citizen of the United States* (New York: Oceana Publications, 1948), p. 75.

12. Jefferson County District Court minutes, November 22, 1873, p. 172.

13. Mittie, Ogden, and Alma lived to adulthood, although Mittie died at age twenty-five in childbirth. See records of Magnolia Cemetery, Beaumont, Tex.

14. J. W. L. Johnson to Sarah Ann Johnson, December 1, 1874. This letter is further quoted below.

15. Jefferson County Commissioners Court minutes, February 1, 1876, vol. D, p. 1; district court records of Will's law examination have not been located.

16. Texas Secretary of State Register of Elected and Appointed Officials, 1874-1878, Texas State Archives, Austin, Texas, pp. 354, 562, shows Will was appointed May 18, 1877; Jefferson County Commissioners Court minutes, vol. D, pp. 48, 55, 73; see also notification in form of letters from W. F. Gilbert to Secretary of State J. G. Searcy, July 24, August 18, 1877.

17. Jefferson County Commissioners Court minutes, vol. D, pp. 19, 55.

18. J. W. L. Johnson to Sarah Ann Johnson, October 10, 1877. This letter is further quoted below.

19. Ibid.

20. Jefferson County Commissioners Court minutes, September 12, 1877, vol. C, pp. 461–62.

21. Ibid.

22. Ibid.

23. John G. Johnson, "Austin State Hospital," in *New Handbook of Texas,* vol. 1, p. 341; Chris Brownson, "From Curer to Custodian: A History of the Texas State Lunatic Asylum, 1857–1880" (master's thesis, University of Texas at Austin, 1992), pp. 26–27; Williams Company, AIA, *A Historic Structure Report: Austin State Hospital Historic Administration Building of 1857* (Austin, Tex.: Williams Co., 1987), pp. 5–6; in 1867, Minerva Hightower, a thirty-five-year-old female, was the first African American to be admitted to the hospital. See, Texas State Lunatic Asylum, admission-discharge ledger, 1861–77, Austin State Hospital, Tex., p. 7.

24. Brownson, "From Curer to Custodian," pp. 16–24; Merle Mears Duncan, "Wallace, David Richard," in *New Handbook of Texas,* vol. 6, p. 805; Doris D. Moore, *The Biography of Doctor D. R. Wallace* (Dallas, Tex.: Timberlawn Foundation, 1966), pp. 8–13; "Mental Illness and Mental Retardation: the History of State Care in Texas," *Impact* [journal of Texas Department of Mental Health and Mental Retardation] 5 (July-August 1975): 5; D. R. Wallace, M.D., ed., *Report of the Board of Managers and Superintendent of the Lunatic Asylum of Texas for the Fiscal Year 1875* (Houston, Tex.: State Printer, A. C. Gray, 1876), p. 19.

25. Texas State Lunatic Asylum, admission-discharge ledger, 1877, p. 24, lists Robert H. Leonard as patient #902; *Houston Daily Post,* November 17, 1880.

26. Mitchell, *Victorian Britain,* p. 747; Earl Wesley Fornell, *The Unhappy Medium* (Austin: University of Texas Press, 1964), pp. 188–220, discusses Lincoln's attendance at seances. Alice Gertrude Leonard's death is noted in *Beaumont News-Beacon,* April 12, 1873.

27. See Leonard, patient #902, Texas State Lunatic Asylum, admission-discharge ledger, 1877; *United States Tenth Census, 1880,* manuscript returns; Leonard, "Uncle Willie's Column," August 12, 1928.

28. Block, *Emerald of the Neches,* pp. 109, 120.

29. Leonard, "Beaumont, Old and New," January 30, 1927.

30. At this time, Will's and Viola's children were Mittie and Ogden; Hannah's and Tom's were Mary, Francis, Frederick, and Kate; and Uncle Bob's and Aunt Rosalie's were Hannah, Clarence, Viola, Robert, and Gertrude (the name Gertrude had been given again, this time to a girl born May 1, 1878). *In the Report of the Board of Managers and Superintendent,* p. 12, Dr. Wallace discusses the social embarrassment associated with mental illness, noting that "friends and family are naturally loath to admit it."

CHAPTER 7

1. Advertisement, *Orange Tribune,* June 6, 1879.

2. Diana J. Kleiner, "Orange, Texas," in *New Handbook of Texas,* vol. 4, pp. 1160–61; Alan S. Mason, "Orange County," in *New Handbook of Texas,* vol. 4, pp. 1161–62; *Orange Tribune,* June 6, 1879, credits the *Houston Telegraph* for Christian's report; railroad schedule in *Beaumont Weekly Lumberman,* April 23, 1880, shows a two-hour travel time to cover the approximate twenty-five miles between Beaumont and Orange. The railroad and sawmill industries of Beaumont, Orange, and Southeast Texas during the postwar years are discussed in Joseph A. Pratt, *The Growth of a Refining Region* (Greenwich, Conn.: JAI Press, 1980), pp. 13–28.

3. *Orange Tribune,* June 6, 1879; Howard C. Williams, ed., *Gateway to Texas: The History of Orange and Orange County* (Orange, Tex.: Heritage House Museum of Orange, 1986), pp. 109–14.

4. John Strickland Spratt, *The Road to Spindletop, Economic Change in Texas, 1875–1901* (1955; reprint, Austin: University of Texas Press, 1970), pp. 256–59; Vera Lee Dugas, "Texas Industry, 1860–1880," *Southwestern Historical Quarterly* 59 (October 1955): 170–73, shows that flour milling ranked first in gross value of production, while lumber milling ranked first in value added; Robert S. Maxwell, "The Pines of Texas, A Study of Lumbering and Public Policy," *East Texas Historical Quarterly* 2 (fall 1964): 77–78; see also Maxwell, "Lumber Industry," in *New Handbook of Texas,* vol. 4, pp. 334–36; *United States Tenth Census, 1880,* Manufactures.

5. *Orange Tribune,* June 6, 1879; Williams, *Gateway to Texas,* p. 98, reports that the Houston-Orange connection was completed in August, 1876, while the *Galveston Daily News* of November 21, 1876, reported that the first excursion train made the trip on November 20; according to Williams, *Gateway to Texas,* pp. 98–99, the Houston-to-New Orleans linkage was finalized July 1, 1881; lumber production statistics from Manufactures, in U.S. ninth (1870) and tenth (1880) censuses, furnished by Jonathan Gerland, Tyrrell Historical Library, Beaumont, Tex.

6. *United States Tenth Census, 1880,* manuscript returns, Orange County, Tex.; *Texas Almanac, 1976–1977* (Dallas, Tex.: A. H. Belo, 1975), pp. 180–86; Maxwell, "Lumber Industry," in *New Handbook of Texas,* vol. 4, pp. 334–36.

7. *United States Tenth Census, 1880,* Orange County, Tex..

8. Ibid.

9. Ibid.; Dibert's resignation is recorded in Texas Register of Elected and Appointed State and County Officials, 1880, Texas State Archives, Austin, reel 70, p. 712; Orange County Commissioners Court minutes, December 21, 1879, Orange County Courthouse, Orange, Tex., records Will Johnson's appointment by Judge Pedigo, also his fellow sureties.

10. Orange County Commissioners Court minutes, December 21, 1879, pp. 120–22; Johnson was succeeded as assessor by A. G. Thomas, Orange County

Commissioners Court minutes, May 16, 1881, pp. 147–49; A. B. Lyons, the assessor elected in 1882, collected a one-year fee of $165.25, according to Orange County Commissioners Court minutes, p. 49.

11. *United States Tenth Census, 1880,* shows Hart age twenty-six, his wife, age twenty-four, and their daughter, age one; Williams, *Gateway to Texas,* p. 239, lists Orange Rifle members, including Johnson, Hart, A. P. Harris, E. I. Kellie, B. H. Norsworthy, Dr. S. W. Sholars, W. H. Stark, John M. Stark, and D. R. Wingate.

12. *Beaumont Enterprise,* December 18, 25, 1880; according to Leonard, *Beaumont Enterprise,* April 30, 1881, the Knights of Honor, which provided $2000 life insurance for each member, was part of a national group that had been founded earlier in Louisville, Kentucky.

13. *United States Tenth Census, 1880.*

14. Orange County District Court records, civil docket, Orange, Tex., pp. 9–17, 25; Orange County Justice Court records, Orange, Tex., pp. 180, 211, 224, 230; *Galveston Weekly News,* December 1, 1881, reports that Sunday laws, requiring closure of all stores including saloons, had been adopted "in nearly every city and large town in Texas."

15. Orange County District Court records, civil docket, pp. 9–17, 25.

16. Orange County District Court records, Patton divorce, file No. 469.

17. Orange County District Court records, minute, motion, and docket books: Sandy Smith, case no. 583, minute books, p. 252; H. McDowell, case no. 577, p. 212; John Hoge, inquest records, pp. 242–44.

18. Jefferson County District Court records, Bullock cases, nos. 638, 639, 640, 641, 645, pp. 372–77; Orange County District Court minutes, Bullock cases, nos. 528–32, pp. 144–52; John W. Leonard to Ogden Johnson, February 15, 1927. Leonard remembered incorrectly that Bullock had been charged with murder.

19. Ibid.

20. Orange County District Court records, including trial and motion dockets, list names of cases and attorneys; Will Johnson's "election" to the bench is recorded in Orange County District Court minutes, April 12, 1880, pp. 282–83.

CHAPTER 8

1. Leonard, "Five Decades Ago in Beaumont."

2. Ibid.

3. Ibid.

4. Leonard, "Uncle Willie's Column," December 2–3, 1928.

5. Ibid.

6. Ibid.

7. Leonard, "Beaumont, Old and New," January 30, 1927.

8. Kate Lamb Mouton, *History of St. Mark's Parish, Beaumont, Texas* (Beaumont: Lamb Printing Co., 1930), p. 11.

9. Lawrence L. Brown, "Protestant Episcopal Church," in *New Handbook of Texas,* vol. 5, pp. 359-61.

10. Lawrence L. Brown, *The Episcopal Church in Texas, 1838-1874* (Austin: The Church Historical Society, 1963), p. 112; Dubose Murphy, *A Short History of the Protestant Episcopal Church* (Dallas, Tex.: Turner Co., 1935), pp. 40-44; William James Battle, "Gregg, Alexander," in *New Handbook of Texas,* vol. 3, pp. 327-28; *United States Eighth Census, 1860,* Travis County, Tex., Slave Inhabitants.

11. James Thayer Addison, *The Episcopal Church in the United States, 1789-1931* (Boston: Archon Books, 1969), pp. 191-93; David Locke, *The Episcopal Church* (New York: Hippocrene Books, 1991), pp. 77-78; Murphy, *Short History of the Protestant Episcopal Church,* pp. 47-50; Raymond W. Albright, *A History of the Protestant Episcopal Church* (New York: MacMillan, 1964), pp. 252-53.

12. Albright, *History of the Protestant Episcopal Church,* pp. 253-54.

13. Murphy, *Short History of the Protestant Episcopal Church,* p. 56; John W. Storey, "Battling Evil: The Growth of Religion in Texas," in *Texas, A Sesquicentennial Celebration,* ed. Donald W. Whisenhunt (Austin, Tex.: Eakin Press, 1984), pp. 377-78.

14. *United States Ninth Census, 1870,* Statistics, pp. 507-18; John W. Storey, "Religion," in *New Handbook of Texas,* vol. 5, pp. 523-29; see also *Journal of the Twenty-first Annual Council of the Protestant Episcopal Church in the Diocese of Texas,* Houston, Tex., 1871. See appendix B in Homer S. Thrall, *History of Methodism in Texas* (Houston, Tex.: E. H. Cushing, 1972), for membership statistics.

15. Brown, *Episcopal Church in Texas, 1838-1874,* pp. 142-43, 249-51.

16. Marguerite Johnston, *A Happy World Abode: Christ Church Cathedral, 1839-1964* (Houston, Tex.: Cathedral Press, 1964), pp. 107-109.

17. Brown, *Episcopal Church in Texas, 1838-1874,* pp. 197-99; Lawrence L. Brown, *The Episcopal Church in Texas, 1875-1965* (Austin, Tex.: The Church Historical Society, 1963), p. 20.

18. *Journal of the Protestant Episcopal Church,* 1876, p. 32; 1877, p. 10; 1878, p. 2.

19. *United States Tenth Census, 1880,* Jefferson County, Tex.

20. Ibid.

21. Leonard, "Uncle Willie's Column," March 24, October 21, 1929; Mouton, *History of St. Mark's,* pp. 4-10.

22. Leonard, "Uncle Willie's Column," October 21, 1929; *United States Tenth Census, 1880,* Jefferson County, Tex.

23. Leonard, "Uncle Willie's Column," October 21, 1929.

24. Ibid.; *Journal of the Protestant Episcopal Church,* 1880, p. 7; Episcopal Diocese Records of Texas, Bishop Alexander Gregg journals, 1877-79, Center for American History, Austin, Tex., pp. 40, 418; Leonard, "Beaumont, Old and New," January 30, 1927. While the Episcopalians were getting organized in Beaumont, other groups thrived in the town. The Methodists, Baptists (including two black congregations), Presbyterians, and Roman Catholics all conducted regular

services there. Jewish people apparently did not hold regular services, but Rosh Hashanah and the ritual closing of their stores were duly noted in the newspaper. See, Block, *Emerald of the Neches,* p. 222.

25. W. D. Sartwelle and Edwin Wickens, eds., *(Waco) Church Bell* [monthly newspaper], April, 1880; Leonard, "Uncle Willie's Column," October 21, 1929.

26. Sartwelle and Wickens, *(Waco) Church Bell,* April, 1880.

27. Leonard, "Uncle Willie's Column," October 21, 1929; *United States Tenth Census, 1880,* Jefferson County, Tex.

28. Block, *Emerald of the Neches,* p. 232. Later, Will's wife, Viola, would be listed as a member of the Beaumont congregation and credited with donating silver spoons to be melted down and cast into the chalice.

29. Rosa Dieu Crenshaw and W. W. Ward, *Cornerstones: A History of Beaumont and Methodism* (Beaumont, Tex.: First Methodist Church Historical Committee, 1968), pp. 30–31.

30. Mouton, *History of St. Mark's,* pp. 4–14; Episcopal Diocese of Texas Records, Bishop Alexander Gregg journals, p. 40. 31. *Journal of the Protestant Episcopal Church,* 1881, pp. 1–3; *United States Tenth Census, 1880.*

31. *Journal of the Protestant Episcopal Church,* 1881, pp. 1–3; United States Tenth Census, 1880.

32. *Journal of the Protestant Episcopal Church,* 1881, pp. 1–3.

33. *Journal of the Protestant Episcopal Church,* 1881, p. 31; Leonard mentions his health problems in Mouton, *History of St. Mark's,* p. 7.

34. *Journal of the Protestant Episcopal Church,* 1881, p. 6.

35. Murphy, *Short History of the Protestant Episcopal Church,* pp. 73–76; Brown, *Episcopal Church in Texas, 1838–1874,* pp. 135–36.

36. J. Carleton Hayden, "After the War: the Mission and Growth of the Episcopal Church among Blacks in the South, 1865–1877," *Historical Magazine of the Protestant Episcopal Church* 42 (December 1973): 403–13; Robert A. Bennett, "Black Episcopalians: A History from the Colonial Period to the Present," *Historical Magazine of the Protestant Episcopal Church* 43 (September 1974): 237–43.

37. *Journal of the Protestant Episcopal Church,* 1881, pp. 29–30.

38. Ibid.

39. Ibid.

40. Ibid.

41. Hayden, "After the War," pp. 403–13; Bennett, "Black Episcopalians," pp. 237–43; Thomas Morton, "A Religious History of Beaumont," *Beaumont Enterprise,* September 18, 1984, pp. 7–8.

42. Mouton, *History of St. Mark's,* p. 13; Leonard, "Uncle Willie's Column," October 21, 1928.

43. Block, *Emerald of the Neches,* p. 234.

44. Ibid.

45. Leonard, "Uncle Willie's Column," October 21, 1928.

46. Mouton, *History of St. Mark's,* p. 8.

47. Leonard, "Uncle Willie's Column," March 24, 1929.

CHAPTER 9

1. Leonard, "Writes His Own Story"; according to W. T. Block, "Early Southeast Texas Newspapers: History of Yesteryear Recorded in Their Yellowed Pages," unpublished MS, author's collection; earlier Beaumont papers included the *Beaumont Banner, Neches Valley News,* and *Beaumont News-Beacon.*

2. Leonard, "Writes His Own Story."

3. Cutrer, *English Texans,* pp. 146–48; Ben C. Stuart, "The History of Texas Newspapers," unpublished MS, Center for American History, Austin, Tex., 1917, pp. 191–98, notes other English Texan newspapermen: Robert Graham Lowe with the *Galveston News* and George Robinson, also with the *Galveston News* and, later, the *Huntsville Weekly Item.*

4. Leonard, "Writes his Own Story."

5. Ibid.; *United States Tenth Census, 1880,* Jefferson County, Tex., #180 (Thackara).

6. Leonard, "Writes his Own Story."

7. Ibid.; *Beaumont Enterprise,* November 6, 1880.

8. *Beaumont Enterprise,* November 6, 1880.

9. Ibid.

10. Ibid.; Grant, who had served two terms, 1868–76, was succeeded by Rutherford B. Hayes, who served one term, 1876–80. The Greenback Party, a group favoring an inflationary monetary policy, flourished briefly among agricultural interests in southern and western states. For discussion of 1880 elections, see Alwyn Barr, *Reconstruction to Reform* (Austin: University of Texas Press, 1971), pp. 59–61.

11. *Beaumont Enterprise,* November 6, 1880.

12. Barr, *Reconstruction to Reform,* pp. 56–61. Democrat Oran M. Roberts first won the governorship in 1878, succeeding Democrat Richard B. Hubbard, who had ascended to the office in 1877, when Richard Coke resigned to take a seat in the U.S. Senate.

13. Statistics about African American workers, from United States ninth (1870) and tenth (1880) censuses, furnished by Jonathan Gerland, Tyrrell Historical Library, Beaumont, Tex.

14. *United States Tenth Census, 1880,* Jefferson County, Tex. In 1860 non-Southerners, many of them railroad workers, made up about 25 percent of the county's population.

15. *Beaumont Enterprise,* December 25, 1880; *Texas Almanac* gives the following 1880 county populations: Jefferson, 3,439; Galveston, 24,121; Harris, 27,985.

16. *Beaumont Enterprise,* December 25, 1880.

17. *Beaumont Enterprise,* July 23, 1881; *United States Tenth Census, 1880,* shows lumber sales of approximately $1 million for Beaumont *and* Orange.

18. Spratt, *Road to Spindletop,* pp. 256–59; John W. Leonard, "Beaumont As I Knew It 50 Years Ago," *Beaumont Enterprise,* date unknown.

19. *Beaumont Enterprise,* January 15, 22, 1881. At first John reported 350 rail cars available, but later reduced it to 280.

20. *Beaumont Enterprise,* December 18, 25, 1880; January 1, 1881. John reported regularly on shallow draft steamboats, such as the *Laura* and the *Van Buskirk,* that operated up and down the Neches River and served Beaumont.

21. *Beaumont Enterprise,* January 8, 22, 1881; a government dredge boat, the *Essayons,* was already dredging the Sabine Pass bar, but John complained about its slow progress in *Beaumont Enterprise,* April 9, 23, 1881.

22. *Beaumont Enterprise,* January 22, 29, February 5, April 9, 1881; Robert Wooster, "Sabine Pass, Texas," in *New Handbook of Texas,* vol. 5, pp. 745–46.

23. *Beaumont Enterprise,* February 5, 12, 1881.

24. *Beaumont Enterprise,* December 18, 25, 1880; February 12, March 19, September 17, 24, 1881.

25. *Beaumont Enterprise,* February 19, March 26, 1881; Leonard, "Beaumont As I Knew It."

26. *Beaumont Enterprise,* April 30, June 25, July 9, 23, 1881. Beaumont had elected a city government in 1860, but it had not been incorporated officially under the laws of the state.

27. *Beaumont Enterprise,* May 28, June 4, July 9, 23, 1881.

28. *Beaumont Enterprise,* July 16, 1881. John Leonard became a naturalized citizen of the United States on October 4, 1876, while living in Arizona.

29. *Beaumont Enterprise,* July 16, 23, 30, August 6, 1881.

30. *Beaumont Enterprise,* August 13, 1881.

31. *Beaumont Enterprise,* November 27, 1880.

32. *Beaumont Enterprise,* August 6, 20, 1881.

33. *Beaumont Enterprise,* January 29, February 26, July 30, 1881.

34. *Beaumont Enterprise,* July 9, 30, August 20, 27, September 24, 1881.

35. *Beaumont Enterprise,* November 6, December 4, 1881. In October 1881 John enrolled Alex Wynne, a Houston printer, as a partner and assigned the Enterprise printing operations to him.

36. *Beaumont Enterprise,* November 20, 27, 1880.

37. James R. Moore, *The Post-Darwinian Controversies: A Study of the Protestant Struggle to Come to Terms with Darwin in Great Britain and America, 1870–1900* (Cambridge: Cambridge University Press, 1979), pp. 217–24, 250–72; John C. Greene, *The Death of Adam* (Ames: Iowa State University Press, 1959), pp. 309–39; Mitchell, *Victorian Britain,* pp. 274–76.

38. *Beaumont Enterprise,* December 18, 1880, February 5, 1881.

39. *Beaumont Enterprise,* November 6, 1880, May 28, October 29, 1881; Leonard, "Uncle Willie's Column," August 3, 1930. The early *Enterprise* comprised four pages with seven columns per page, a total of twenty-eight columns available for news or advertising.

40. *Beaumont Enterprise,* February 5, April 30, May 21, 1881; Louise C. Allen, Ernest A. Sharpe, and John R. Whitaker, "Newspapers," in *New Handbook of Texas,* vol. 4, pp. 1000–1002; Thomas W. Cutrer, "McGary, Dan H.," in *New Handbook of Texas,* vol. 4, p. 401; Ernest Speck, "Newcomb, James Pearson," in *New Handbook of Texas,* vol. 4, pp. 898–90; Dugas, "Texas Industry," *Southwestern Historical Quarterly* 59 (October 1955): 177.

41. *Beaumont Enterprise,* May 21, 1881; "Sweet, George H.," in *New Handbook of Texas,* vol. 6, pp. 171–72.

42. *Beaumont Enterprise,* November 13, 1880.

43. Ibid.; *Beaumont Enterprise,* January 29, 1881.

44. *Beaumont Enterprise,* August 6, 13, 27, 1881; *Galveston Daily News,* August 20, 27, 1881; *Houston Daily Post,* August 20, 23, 1881; Williams, *Gateway to Texas,* pp. 60–61, reports that six African Americans were killed.

45. *Houston Daily Post,* August 20, 23, 1881.

46. *Beaumont Enterprise,* August 6, 1881.

CHAPTER 10

1. *Beaumont Enterprise,* October 29, 1881.

2. Ibid.

3. Ibid.; Orange County District Court minutes, vol. D, pp. 328, 372, 411; *Texas Statutes* (Vernon, 1936), art. 1427, secs. 1346, 875, 741.

4. Orange County District Court minutes, vol. D, pp. 487–88.

5. Doris Cowart to Robert J. Robertson, date unknown.

6. Orange County District Court minutes, p. 490.

7. Orange County District Court minutes, vol. E, p. 31.

8. Leonard, "Writes his Own Story"; Leonard, "Beaumont, Old and New," January 30, 1927; Frank Spurgeon Morris, "History of the *Beaumont Enterprise*" (master's thesis, Stephen F. Austin College, 1962), p. 12.

9. Orange County District Court minutes, vol. E, p. 44.

10. J. W. L. Johnson to Viola Johnson, October 16, 1882. Letter quoted here and in subsequent paragraphs.

11. J. W. L. Johnson to Viola Johnson, October 29, 1882. Letter quoted here and in subsequent paragraphs.

12. Information about the nature of the Sabine Pass "brush contract" furnished by local historian, W. D. Quick, Nederland, Tex.

13. Cowart to Robertson, December 1, 1996, author's collection.

EPILOGUE

1. *New York Herald Tribune,* July 2, 1932; *Brooklyn Daily Eagle,* July 3, 1932; biographic outlines, prepared by Howard E. Tompkins, John W. Leonard's grandson, author's collection.

2. Tompkins, biographic outlines.

3. Ibid.

4. *New York Herald Tribune,* June 6, 1932.

5. *New York Herald Tribune,* July 2, 1932; *Brooklyn Daily Eagle,* July 3, 1932; Tompkins, biographic outlines.

6. "Uncle Willie's" columns are found in the Sunday edition of the *Beaumont Enterprise,* beginning May 13, 1928, and running four years.

7. *New York Herald Tribune,* June 6, July 2, 1932.

8. *Beaumont Enterprise,* July 2, 1932; *New York Herald Tribune,* July 2, 1932; *Brooklyn Times Herald,* July 2, 1932; *Brooklyn Daily Eagle,* July 2, 3, 1932; *New York Evening Post,* July 2, 1932.

9. Robert H. Leonard died February 19, 1892. *Houston Daily Post,* February 20, 21, 1892. Jefferson County deed records show Robert H. Leonard engaged in dozens of land transactions, commencing in 1859 and ending 1892.

10. Thomas A. Lamb died August 29, 1917. *Beaumont Enterprise,* August 30, 1917.

11. *Beaumont Journal,* September 12, 1923; "pioneer of the city" from *Beaumont Enterprise,* September 13, 1923.

12. John W. Leonard to Ogden Johnson, February 15, 1927. Viola Johnson's death and John Leonard's visit to Beaumont are reported in the *Beaumont Enterprise,* January 20, 1927.

13. Doris Lawhon Cowart, adopted daughter of Alma, provided the author with information about this period in Viola's life. The author concludes that an estrangement between Viola and her brothers is the most logical explanation for her hard times. That bad feelings existed between Viola and her brothers is further supported by family lore, which holds that Lem and Ed Ogden drove Will away, threatening to kill him. The family story, passed down to Doris L. Cowart and, separately, to the author, did not include reasons why the brothers would take such action.

14. Cowart to Robertson.

15. Divorce record no. 1021, Jefferson County District Clerk, Jefferson County Courthouse, Beaumont, Tex.; Viola was represented by Douglas, Lanier & Bullitt; Will's court-appointed attorneys were O'Brien & John. The August 1, 1882, date of abandonment cited in the petition is an obvious and apparently innocent error, given that Viola had Will's letters postmarked in Orange and Beaumont in October of that year.

16. Jefferson County deed records show various land transactions involving Viola C. Johnson, both as grantor and grantee, beginning in 1895.

17. Jefferson County marriage records, no. 1759A, vol. 3, p. 5; clippings, *Beaumont Enterprise,* dates unknown. The newspaper article about Mittie's death does not mention the child birth, but an unnamed infant is buried next to her.

18. Jefferson County, subdivision maps, Johnson Addition, filed by Viola C. Ogden, July 1, 1901.

19. "Sabine Oaks" article in *Beaumont Enterprise,* August 4, 1957, describes the Johnson residence, sketches its history, and features a photograph of it. The house is shown on various Sanborn maps, Tyrrell Historical Library, Beaumont.

20. Ogden Johnson, then Jefferson County tax assessor, married Lomie Salter on August 25, 1901. Jefferson County marriage records; *Beaumont Enterprise,* March 31, 1961.

21. Jefferson County deed records, file #20409, vol. 91, pp. 241-42, show sale of Viola C. Johnson homestead to W. D. Myers for $10,250; various Beaumont city directories, 1904-1905, 1909, 1910-11, 1912-13, 1916, 1921-22, 1925-26, Tyrrell Historical Library, show Viola first living with son Ogden, then by 1921 with daughter Alma.

22. Beaumont city directory, 1921-22, Tyrrell Historical Library, shows Viola residing at 2244 Liberty with I. W. and Alma Lawhon. The Lawhons adopted a second child, Joe, born May 10, 1909, and taken to their home three days later. Doris Lawhon Cowart to Robertson, concerning Viola's room with seven windows and her last months.

23. *Beaumont Enterprise,* January 20, 1927; *Beaumont Journal,* January 20, 1927; Jefferson County probate records, File No. 3207.

24. David McCullough, *The Path between the Seas: The Creation of the Panama Canal, 1870-1914* (New York: Simon and Schuster, 1977), pp. 101-203, discusses the de Lesseps phase of the project. See also, Miles P. DuVal, Jr., *And the Mountains Will Move: The Story of the Building of the Panama Canal* (London: Oxford University Press, 1947), pp. 67-128; Ulrich Keller, *The Building of the Panama Canal in Historic Photographs* (New York: Dover Publications, 1983), pp. v-vi, 1-4; Ira E. Bennett, *History of the Panama Canal: Its Construction and Builders* (Washington, D.C.: Historical Publishing Co., 1915), pp. 101-102.

25. McCullough, *Path between the Seas,* pp. 145-47, 170-75.

26. Ibid., pp. 145-47; *Bakersfield Morning Echo,* March 10, 1904.

27. *Bakersfield Daily Californian,* March 19, 1904.

28. *Ventura Free Press,* August 1, 1890.

29. Ibid., January 13, 1891.

30. *Bakersfield Daily Californian,* January 6, 1892; March 19, 1904; *Ventura Free Press,* April 19, 1895.

31. *Bakersfield Daily Californian,* January 13, 1892.

32. California Great Register, 1892-93, Kern County, item #3339; *Bakersfield Daily Californian,* January 5, 1892; *Bakersfield Morning Echo,* March 10, 1904.

33. *Bakersfield Morning Echo,* March 10, 1904.

34. *Ventura Free Press,* April 19, 1895.

35. *Bakersfield Daily Californian,* March 19, 1904.

36. Bureau of the Census, *United States Twelfth Census, 1900,* California, Ventura County, Inhabitants.

37. *Bakersfield Daily Californian,* March 19, 1904.

38. Ibid.

39. Ogden Johnson's brutal rejection of his father's message is part of family lore as passed down and told to the author. *Bakersfield Daily Californian,* March 19, 1904.

40. *Santa Barbara Morning Press,* March 6, 1904.

41. *Bakersfield Daily Californian,* March 19, 1904.

42. Ibid.

BIBLIOGRAPHY

UNPUBLISHED SOURCES

Austin State Hospital, Austin, Tex. Texas State Lunatic Asylum admission-discharge register. 1861–77.

Baggett, James Alex. "The Rise and Fall of the Texas Radicals, 1867–1883." Ph.D. diss., North Texas State University, 1972.

Block, W. T. "Early Beaumont Education: Frontier Schools Provided the City's Leaders of the Future." MS. Author's collection.

———. "Early Southeast Texas Newspapers: History of Yesteryear Recorded in Their Yellowed Pages." MS. Author's collection.

Brownson, Chris. "From Curer to Custodian: A History of the Texas State Lunatic Asylum, 1857–1880." Master's thesis, University of Texas at Austin, 1992.

California Great Register, 1892–93. Beal Memorial Library, Bakersfield, Calif.

Campbell, Randolph B. "Grass Roots Reconstruction in Texas: An Overview." MS. 1994. Author's collection.

Carrier, John P. "A Political History of Texas during the Reconstruction, 1867–1874." Ph.D. diss., Vanderbilt University, 1971.

Cowart, Doris Lawhon. Letter to author, December 1, 1996. Author's collection.

Freeman, Mary Helen Hatchell. "East Texas, A Social and Economic History of the Counties East of the Trinity River, 1850–1860." Master's thesis, Lamar University, 1976.

Gilbert, W. F. Letters to Secretary of State J. G. Searcy, July 24, August 18, 1877. Jefferson County Clerk office, Beaumont, Tex.

Hardin County District Court minutes index, Kountze, Tex.

Jefferson County Commissioners Court minutes. Jefferson County Courthouse, Beaumont, Tex.

Jefferson County District Court minutes. Jefferson County Courthouse, Beaumont, Tex.

Jefferson County marriage records. Jefferson County Courthouse, Beaumont, Tex.

Johnson, J. W. L. Letters. Author's collection.

Johnson, Sarah Ann. Letters. Author's collection.

Lamb, Hannah Leonard. Diary. Author's collection.

Lamb, Thomas A. Texas teacher's certificate. Author's collection.

Leonard, John W. Papers and letters. Author's collection.

Leonard, Robert H. Letters. Author's collection.

Mathews, Clarke A. "History of the Schools of Jefferson County to 1883." Master's thesis, University of Texas, 1937.

Morris, Frank Spurgeon, "History of the *Beaumont Enterprise.*" Master's thesis, Stephen F. Austin State College, 1962.

Office of Population Censuses and Surveys, London. Census and Birth Records.

Orange County District Court records. Orange County Clerk office, Orange, Tex.; Sam Houston Regional Library, Liberty, Tex.

Richards, Paul. Letter to author, January 27, 1995. Author's collection.

Smith, Stewart D. "Schools and Schoolmen: Chapters in Texas Education." Ph.D. diss., North Texas State University, 1974.

Stuart, Ben C. "The History of Texas Newspapers." MS. 1917. Center for American History, Austin, Tex.

Texas Secretary of State. Texas Register of Elected and Appointed State and County Officials, 1874–80. Texas State Archives, Austin.

United Kingdom. Newcastle Commission, Report, 1858. The British and Foreign School Society Archives Centre, London.

United States Eighth Census, 1860. Manuscript returns. Microfilm copies, Tyrrell Historical Library, Beaumont, Tex.

United States Ninth Census, 1870. Manuscript returns. Microfilm copies, Tyrrell Historical Library, Beaumont, Tex.

United States Tenth Census, 1880. Manuscript returns. Microfilm copies, Tyrrell Historical Library, Beaumont, Tex.

United States Twelfth Census, 1900. Manuscript returns. Microfilm copies, Tyrrell Historical Library, Beaumont, Tex.

White, Anita Louise. "The Teacher in Texas: 1836–1879." Ed.D. diss., Baylor University, 1979.

White, Michael Allen. "History of Education in Texas, 1860–1884." Ed.D. diss., Baylor University, 1969.

Williams, Patrick George. "Redeemer Democrats and the Roots of Modern Texas, 1872–1884." Ph.D. diss., Columbia University, 1996.

PUBLISHED SOURCES

Addison, James Thayer. *The Episcopal Church in the United States, 1789–1931.* Boston: Archon Books, 1969.

Adsman, John William. *English Education, 1789–1902.* Cambridge: Cambridge University Press, 1930.

Albright, Raymond W. *A History of the Protestant Episcopal Church.* New York: MacMillan, 1964.

Altick, Richard D. *Victorian People and Ideas.* New York: W. W. Norton, 1973.

BIBLIOGRAPHY

Ashford, Gerald. "Jacksonian Liberalism and Spanish Law in Early Texas." *Southwestern Historical Quarterly* 57 (July 1953): 1–37.

Baines, Dudley. *Migration in a Mature Economy*. Cambridge: Cambridge University Press, 1985.

Barr, Alwyn. *Black Texans: A History of Negroes in Texas, 1528–1971*. Austin, Tex.: Jenkins Publishing Co., 1982.

———. *Reconstruction to Reform, Texas Politics, 1876–1906*. Austin: University of Texas Press, 1971.

Baughman, James P. "The Evolution of Rail-Water Systems of Transportation in the Gulf-Southwest, 1836–1890." *Journal of Southern History* 34 (August 1968): 357–81.

Beales, Derek. *From Castlereagh to Gladstone, 1815–1885*. New York: Norton, 1969.

Bennett, Ira E. *History of the Panama Canal: Its Construction and Builders*. Washington D. C.: Historical Publishing Co., 1915.

Bennett, Robert A. "Black Episcopalians: A History from the Colonial Period to the Present." *Historical Magazine of the Protestant Episcopal Church* 43 (September 1974): 231–45.

Bentley and Pilgrim [law firm], ed. *Texas Legal Directory*. Austin: Democratic Statesman Office, 1877.

Best, Geoffrey. *Mid-Victorian Britain, 1851–1875*. New York: Schoechen Books, 1972.

Betjeman, John. *Victorian and Edwardian London from Old Photographs*. New York: Viking Press, 1967.

Biographical Directory of Texas Conventions and Congresses, 1832–1845. Reprint, St. Augustine, Tex.: S. Malone, 1986.

Black, Eugene C. *Victorian Culture and Society*. New York: Walker and Co., 1974.

Block, W. T., ed. "Beaumont in the 1850s: Excerpts from the Writings of Henry R. Green." *Texas Gulf Historical and Biographical Record* 11 (November 1975): 49–78.

———. *Emerald of the Neches: The Chronicles of Beaumont, Texas, From Reconstruction to Spindletop*. Nederland, Tex.: W. T. Block, 1980.

Bolt, Christine. *Victorian Attitudes to Race*. London: Routledge and Kegan Paul, 1971.

Boner, Marian. *A Reference Guide to Texas Law and Legal History*. Austin: University of Texas Press, 1976.

Brewer, J. Mason. *Negro Legislators of Texas*. Austin, Tex.: Jenkins Publishing Co., 1970.

Briggs, Asa. *A Social History of England*. New York: Viking Press, 1983.

———. *Victorian Cities*. New York: Harper and Row, 1963.

———. *Victorian People: A Reassessment of Persons and Themes, 1851–1867*. New York: Harper and Row, 1955.

Brown, Lawrence L. *The Episcopal Church in Texas, 1875–1965*. Austin, Tex.: Eakin Press, 1985.

———. *The Episcopal Church in Texas, 1838–1874.* Austin, Tex.: The Church Historical Society, 1963.

Burn, W. L. *The Age of Equipoise: A Study of the Mid-Victorian Generation.* London: George Allen and Unwin, 1964.

Burnham, Eleanor D., ed. *Subject Catalogue of the Special Panama Collection of the Canal Zone Library-Museum.* Boston: G. K. Hall and Co., 1964.

Calvert, Robert A., and Arnoldo DeLeon. *The History of Texas.* Arlington Heights, Ill.: Harland Davis, 1990.

Campbell, Randolph B. "Carpetbagger Rule in Reconstruction Texas: An Enduring Myth." *Southwestern Historical Quarterly* 97 (April 1994): 587–97.

———. "George W. Whitmore: East Texas Unionist." *East Texas Historical Journal* 28, no. 1 (spring 1990): 17–28.

———. "Reconstruction in Jefferson County, 1865–1876." *Texas Gulf Historical and Biographical Record* 31 (November 1995): 10–28.

———. *A Southern Community in Crisis: Harrison County, Texas, 1850–1880.* Austin: Texas State Historical Association, 1983.

———. "Statehood, Civil War, and Reconstruction, 1846–1876." In *Texas through Time: Evolving Interpretations,* edited by Walter L. Buenger and Robert A. Calvert. College Station: Texas A&M University Press, 1991.

Campbell, Randolph B., and Richard G. Lowe. *Wealth and Power in Antebellum Texas.* College Station: Texas A&M University Press, 1977.

Clemenceau, Georges. *American Reconstruction, 1865–1870.* Edited by Fernand Baldensperger. New York: Lincoln McVeigh-The Dial Press, 1928.

Congressional Research Service, Library of Congress. *A Chronology of Events Relating to Panama Canal.* Washington, D.C.: Government Printing Office, 1977.

Crenshaw, Rosa Dieu, and W. W. Ward. *Cornerstones: A History of Beaumont and Methodism.* Beaumont, Tex.: First Methodist Church Historical Committee, 1968.

Crouch, Barry A. "All the Vile Passions: The Texas Black Code of 1866." *Southwestern Historical Quarterly* 97 (July 1993): 13–34.

———. "The Freedmen's Bureau in Beaumont." Parts 1 and 2. *Texas Gulf Historical and Biographical Record* 28 (November 1992): 8–27; 29 (November 1993): 8–29.

———. "Guardian of the Freedpeople: Texas Freedmen's Bureau Agents and the Black Community." *Southern Studies* 3 (fall 1992): 185–201.

———. "Hidden Sources of Black History: The Texas Freedmen's Bureau Records as a Case Study." *Southwestern Historical Quarterly* 83 (January 1980): 211–26.

Crouch, Barry A., and Leon J. Schultz. "Crisis in Color: Racial Separation in Texas during Reconstruction." *Civil War History* 16 (March 1970): 37–49.

Curtis, Stanley James. *History of Education in Great Britain.* London: University Tutorial Press, 1953.

Cutrer, Thomas W. *The English Texans.* San Antonio: Institute of Texan Cultures, 1985.

Doubleday, H. Arthur, ed. *The Victoria History of the Counties of England: A History of Norfolk.* Reprint, Folkstone, Kent, U.K.: William Dawson and Sons, 1975.

Dugas, Vera Lee. "Texas Industry, 1860–1880." *Southwestern Historical Quarterly* 59 (October 1955): 151–83.

DuVal, Miles P., Jr. *And the Mountains Will Move: The Story of the Building of the Panama Canal.* London: Oxford University Press, 1947.

Eby, Frederick. *The Development of Education in Texas.* New York: MacMillan, 1925.

Erickson, Charlotte. "English." In *Harvard Encyclopedia of American Ethnic Groups,* edited by Stephen Thernstrom. Cambridge, Mass.: Harvard University Press, 1980.

———. *Invisible Immigrants, the Adaptation of English and Scottish Immigrants in Nineteen-Century America.* Coral Gables, Fla.: University of Miami Press, 1972.

———. *Leaving England: Essays on British Emigration in the Nineteenth Century.* Ithaca, N.Y.: Cornell University Press, 1994.

Evans, C. E. *The Story of Texas Schools.* Austin, Tex.: Steck Co., 1955.

Fletcher, William A. *Rebel Private: Front and Rear.* New York: Dutton, 1995.

Foner, Eric. *Reconstruction, America's Unfinished Revolution, 1863–1877.* New York: Harper and Row, 1988.

Fornell, Earl Wesley. *The Galveston Era.* Austin: University of Texas Press, 1961.

———. *The Unhappy Medium.* Austin: University of Texas Press, 1964.

Franklin, Frank George. *The Legislative History of Naturalization in the United States.* New York: Arno Press, 1969.

Gordon, Milton M. *Assimilation in American Life.* New York: Oxford University Press, 1964.

Gray, Robert. *A History of London.* New York: Dorset Press, 1978.

Greene, John C. *The Death of Adam.* Ames: Iowa State University Press, 1959.

Gregg, Wilson. *Alexander Gregg, First Bishop of Texas.* Sewanee, Tenn.: The University Press, 1912.

Hall, Margaret E. *How To Become a Citizen of the United States.* New York: Oceana Publications, 1948.

Hayden, J. Carleton. "After the War: The Mission and Growth of the Episcopal Church among Blacks in the South, 1865–1877." *Historical Magazine of the Protestant Episcopal Church* 42 (December 1975): 403–27.

Hornsby, Alton, Jr. "The Freedmen's Bureau Schools in Texas, 1865–1870." *Southwestern Historical Quarterly* 76 (April 1973): 397–99.

Houghton, Walter E. *The Victorian Frame of Mind.* New Haven, Conn.: Yale University Press, 1957.

Hurt, John. *Education in Evolution: Church, State, Society and Popular Education, 1800–1870.* London: Rupert Hart-Davis, 1971.

Johnston, Marguerite. *A Happy World Abode: Christ Church Cathedral, 1839–1964.* Houston, Tex.: Cathedral Press, 1964.

Journal of the Thirty-Second Annual Council of the Protestant Episcopal Church. Houston, Tex. (1881).

Journal of the Twenty-First Annual Council of the Protestant Episcopal Church. Houston, Tex. (1871).

Keller, Ulrich. *The Building of the Panama Canal in Historic Photographs.* New York: Dover Publications, 1983.

Kelly, E. B., ed. *Post Office Directory of Norfolk.* Norwich, U.K.: Kelly and Company, 1858 and 1865 eds.

Kerr, Homer L. "Migration into Texas, 1860–1880." *Southwestern Historical Quarterly* 70 (October 1966): 184–216.

Kettner, James H. *The Development of American Citizenship, 1608–1870.* Chapel Hill: University of North Carolina Press, 1978.

Konolige, Kit, and Frederica Konolige. *The Power of Their Glory. America's Ruling Class: The Episcopalians.* New York: Wyden Books, 1978.

Lasswell, Mary. *John Henry Kirby: Prince of the Pines.* Austin, Tex.: Encino Press, 1967.

Ledbetter, Billy D. "White Texans' Attitudes toward the Political Equality of Negroes, 1865–1870." *Phylon* 40 (September 1979): 253–63.

Leonard, Thomas M. *Panama, the Canal and the United States: A Guide to Issues and References.* Claremont, Calif.: Regina Books, 1993.

Linsley, Judith W., and Ellen W. Rienstra. *Beaumont: A Chronicle of Promise.* Woodland Hills, Calif.: Windsor Publications, 1982.

Locke, David. *The Episcopal Church.* New York: Hippocrene Books, 1991.

Lynch, James D. *The Bench and Bar of Texas.* St. Louis, Mo.: Nixon-Jones Printing Co., 1885.

Markham, Edward L. "Reception of the Common Law of England in Texas and Judicial Attitudes toward That Reception, 1840–1859." *Texas Law Review* 29 (October 1951): 904–30.

Maxwell, Robert S. "The Pines of Texas, A Study of Lumbering and Public Policy." *East Texas Historical Quarterly* 2 (fall 1964): 77–86.

McCullough, David. *The Path between the Seas: The Creation of the Panama Canal, 1870–1914.* New York: Simon and Schuster, 1977.

Men of Texas. Houston, Tex.: Houston Post, 1903.

"Mental Illness and Mental Retardation: the History of State Care in Texas." *Impact* [journal of Texas Department of Mental Health and Mental Retardation] 5 (July–August 1975): 3–6.

Mitchell, Sally, ed. *Victorian Britain.* New York: Garland Publishing, 1988.

Moneyhon, Carl H. "Public Education and Texas Reconstruction Politics, 1871–1874." *Southwestern Historical Quarterly* 94 (January 1989): 393–416.

———. *Republicanism in Reconstruction Texas.* Austin: University of Texas Press, 1980.

Moore, Doris D. *The Biography of Doctor D. R. Wallace.* Dallas, Tex.: Timberlawn Foundation, 1966.

Moore, James R. *The Post-Darwinian Controversies: A Study of the Protestant Struggle to Come to Terms with Darwin in Great Britain and America, 1870–1900.* Cambridge: Cambridge University Press, 1979.

Morgan, Kenneth O., ed. *The Oxford Illustrated History of Britain.* Oxford: Oxford University Press, 1984.

Morton, Thomas. "A Religious History of Beaumont." *Beaumont Enterprise,* September 18, 1984, pp. 2–8.

Mouton, Kate Lamb. *History of St. Mark's Parish, Beaumont, Texas.* Beaumont: Lamb Printing Co., 1930.

Murphy, Dubose. *A Short History of the Protestant Episcopal Church.* Dallas, Tex.: Turner Co., 1935.

Nunn, W. C. *Texas under the Carpetbaggers.* Austin: University of Texas Press, 1962.

Olmsted, Frederick Law. *A Journey through Texas; or a Saddletrip on the Southwestern Frontier.* Austin: University of Texas Press, 1978.

Perrott, Vera. *Victoria's Lynn, Boom & Prosperity.* Seaford, U.K.: Vista Books, 1995.

Planck, Lewis H., ed. *Planck's Texas Legal Directory.* Gonzales, Tex.: Lewis H. Planck, 1882.

Pratt, Joseph A. *The Growth of a Refining Region.* Greenwich, Conn.: JAI Press, 1980.

Radley, Kenneth. *Rebel Watchdog, The Confederate States Army Provost Guard.* Baton Rouge: Louisiana State University Press, 1989.

Ragan, Cooper K., ed. "The Diary of Captain O'Brien, 1863." *Southwestern Historical Quarterly* 67 (July 1963): 28–54; (October 1963): 235–46.

Ramsdell, Charles W. *Reconstruction in Texas.* New York: Columbia University, 1910.

Rice, Lawrence D. *The Negro in Texas, 1874–1900.* Baton Rouge: Louisiana State University Press, 1971.

Richards, Paul. *King's Lynn.* Chichester, U.K.: Phillimore, 1990.

Richter, William L. *The Army in Texas During Reconstruction, 1865–1870.* College Station: Texas A&M University Press, 1987.

———. *Overreached on All Sides: The Freedmen's Bureau Administrators in Texas, 1865–1868.* College Station: Texas A&M University Press, 1991.

Robertson, Robert J. "Beaumont on the Eve of the Civil War, As Seen in *The Beaumont Banner.*" *Texas Gulf Historical and Biographical Record* 30 (November 1994): 8–26.

BIBLIOGRAPHY

———. "Slavery and the Coming of the Civil War, As Seen in *The Beaumont Banner.*" *East Texas Historical Journal* 34, no. 1 (spring 1996): 14–29.

Russ, William R., Jr. "Radical Disfranchisement in Texas, 1867–1870." *Southwestern Historical Quarterly* 38 (July 1934): 40–52.

Russell, Traylor, ed. *Centennial History of the Texas Bar.* Austin, Tex.: Eakin Press, 1981.

Schaadt, Robert L. *The History of Hardin County.* Kountze, Tex.: Hardin County Historical Commission, 1991.

Seaman, L. C. B. *Life in Victorian London.* London: B. T. Batsford, 1973.

Shepperson, Wilbur S. *Emigration and Disenchantment.* Norman: University of Oklahoma Press, 1965.

Sibley, Marilyn M. *Lone Stars and State Gazettes: Texas Newspapers before the Civil War.* College Station: Texas A&M University Press, 1983.

Simpson, Harold B. *Hood's Texas Brigade: A Compendium.* Hillsboro, Tex.: Hill Jr. College Series, 1977.

Smallwood, James. "Black Education in Reconstruction Texas: The Contributions of the Freedmen's Bureau and Benevolent Societies." *East Texas Historical Journal* 19 (spring 1981): 17–35.

———. *Time of Hope, Time of Despair, Black Texans During Reconstruction.* Port Washington, N.Y.: Kennikat Press, 1981.

Spratt, John Strickland. *The Road to Spindletop, Economic Change in Texas, 1875–1901.* 1955. Reprint, Austin: University of Texas Press, 1970.

State of Texas against William Chambers, Judge First Judicial District, before the Senate of the Fourteenth Legislature, Sitting as a High Court of Impeachment. Austin: Cardwell and Walker, 1874.

Storey, John W. "Battling Evil: The Growth of Religion in Texas." In *Texas, A Sesquicentennial Celebration,* edited by Donald W. Whisenhunt. Austin: Eakin Press, 1984.

Texas Statutes. Kansas City, Mo.: Vernon, 1936.

Thompson, F. M. L. *The Rise of Respectable Society: A Social History of Victorian Britain, 1830–1900.* Cambridge, Mass.: Harvard University Press, 1988.

Thrall, Homer S. *History of Methodism in Texas.* Houston, Tex.: E. H. Cushing, 1872.

Tyler, Ron C., et al., eds. *The New Handbook of Texas.* Austin: Texas State Historical Association, 1996.

Wallace, D. R., M.D. *Report of the Board of Managers and Superintendent of the Lunatic Asylum of Texas for the Fiscal Year 1875.* Houston, Tex.: State Printer, A. C. Gray, 1876.

———. *Report of the Board of Managers of the State Lunatic Asylum of Texas for the Fiscal Year 1877–78.* Austin: Institution for the Deaf and the Dumb, 1878.

Webb, Walter P., et al., eds. *Handbook of Texas.* Austin: Texas State Historical Association, 1952.

Weinreb, Ben, and Christopher Hibbert, eds. *The London Encyclopedia*. Bethesda, Md.: Adler and Adler, 1972.

White, William, ed. *History, Gazetteer and Directory of Norfolk*. King's Lynn, U.K.: White and Company, 1864.

Williams, Howard C., ed. *Gateway to Texas: The History of Orange and Orange County*. Orange, Tex.: Heritage House Museum of Orange, 1986.

Williams Company, AIA. *A Historic Structure Report: Austin State Hospital Historic Administration Building of 1857*. Austin, Tex.: Williams Co., 1987.

Wilson, J. Dover, ed. *The Schools of England*. Chapel Hill: University of North Carolina Press, 1929.

Wintz, Cary D. *Texas Politics in the Gilded Age, 1873–1890*. Boston: American Press, 1983.

Woodward, Sir Llewellyn. *The Age of Reform, 1815–1870*. Oxford: Oxford University Press, 1962.

Wooster, Ralph A. "Foreigners in the Principal Towns of Ante-Bellum Texas." *Southwestern Historical Quarterly* 65 (October 1962): 208–20.

———. *People in Power, Courthouse and Statehouse in the Lower South, 1850–1860*. Knoxville: University of Tennessee Press, 1969.

———. *The Secession Conventions of the South*. Princeton, N.J.: Princeton University Press, 1962.

Index

Pages containing illustrations appear in italics.